Coming Home
to South Omaha

Coming Home
to South Omaha

An Immigrant Family's Journey
From Ireland & Scotland to Nebraska

David J. Krajicek

News Ink Books

News Ink Books

Copyright 2022 by David J. Krajicek

ISBN 978-0-9849036-1-0

Original Drawings by Karen Gutliph Graves

Cover Painting by Edward L. Krajicek Jr.

Book Design by Terry Bradshaw

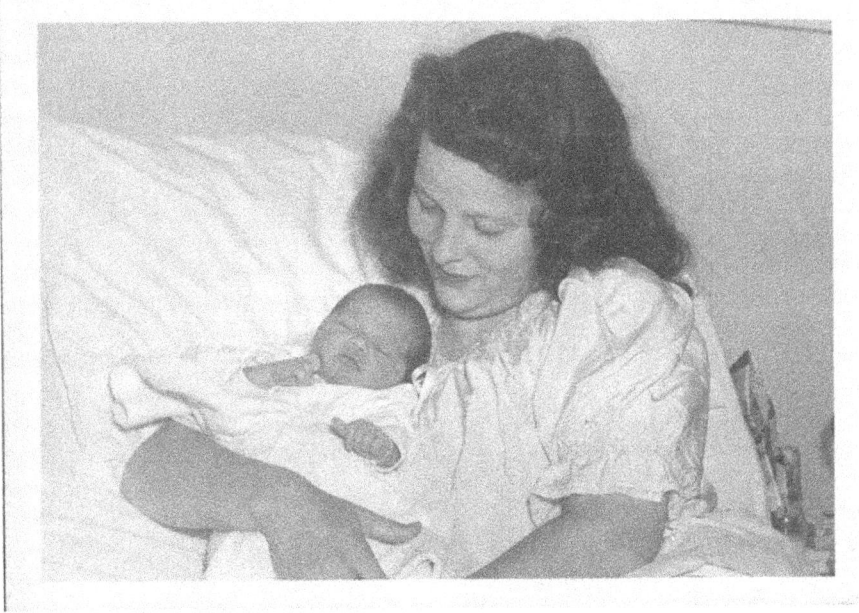

Helen Strack Krajicek

*This deep look into my maternal ancestry
was inspired by memories of my mother,
Helen Marie Strack Krajicek.*

*This book is for her,
a woman who gave her life to her children.*

Painted by Edward L. Krajicek Jr. in about 1980

Contents

ONE

Beginnings

ON A SUMMER DAY nearly 150 years ago, a thin young Irishwoman, hauling two bags that contained everything she owned, made her way down a crowded steamship gangplank onto a bustling dock at Long Wharf in Boston Harbor. Her name was Ellen McAuliffe, known to her loved ones as Nellie. She was 20 years old and hailed from Limerick, an ancient city in the Mid-West of Ireland. On that day, July 7, 1883, Nellie took her first steps on American soil. She was in the midst of a journey that would lead to South Omaha, Nebraska, 4,000 miles from home. There, she would put down new roots and eventually become matriarch of a vast immigrant family that within a few generations numbered in the hundreds.

Nellie McAuliffe was my maternal great-grandmother, my mother's mother's mother. This is her story — and ours, her American descendants with a hodgepodge of European surnames, including Kinnear, Kleber, Bogatz, Strack, Dundis, Krajicek, Keating, and dozens of others. In this book, I have tried to create an accurate account of the lives of Nellie and her Scottish-born husband, William Kinnear, as well as their forebears in Europe and immediate descendants here in the United States, including my grandmother (and Nellie's daughter), Eileen Kinnear Strack. I hope it serves as a lasting record of who we are and where we came from. I encourage the individual families of our relatives to append to my account their own records of subsequent generations.

As with most families, our first generation of immigrants were concerned with survival in their adopted homeland. That means they got up in the morning and went to work. Across all races, ethnicities, and national origins, these first-generation newcomers tend to look forward, not back. Often, it is up to subsequent generations to learn, record, and tell their ancestors' origin stories. Left untold, these tales are lost forever when our elders leave us. So record them now, before it's too late.

This process is so much easier today, with smart phones that function as video production studios, and endless academic and government resources with tips on gathering immigrant stories. Unfortunately, none of this was available in the time of our Nellie and William, nor did these two seem inclined to leave much of an accounting — written or oral — about their lives in the Old Country. So much of what I was able to learn about them, beyond a handful of news clippings and a sheaf of government documents, has come to me third-hand. And like the old telephone game, these passed-along stories can morph in the retelling. Gauzy details fade even further with the passage of time, and questionable fables can become firm facts in family lore.

Another factor in our family's loss of shared history is what I've come to think of as genealogical sprawl. This family got very big very quickly, kind of like those endless suburban subdivisions that continue to leapfrog themselves in the ever-expanding residential rings on southern and western flanks of Omaha, my hometown. We had so many first cousins, who could keep track of second cousins?

As my research on this book was nearing its end, I was telling my older sister, Colleen Krajicek, about the life and tragic death of one of our grandmother's sisters. Colleen asked a good question: "Why

2

didn't we know these people?" I think the answer, in part, is our genealogical sprawl. We were Catholics who procreated enthusiastically. Great-grandmother Nellie had six children. My grandmother had five. My mother, Helen, had eight kids, and her younger sister Eileen had seven. Their older sister Dorothy and brother George had five each, and their fifth sibling, Bud Strack, had four. Family gatherings that were limited to just these first cousins could include nearly thirty children. (Yes, it was bedlam.) We had little contact with the abundant throng of our second cousins—the Klebers of South Omaha, for example, whose matron was my grandmother's oldest sister.

Every few years, Grandma Strack and her siblings would call the Kinnear tribe together for a full reunion picnic at Spring Lake Park in South Omaha. Half of this crowd, as many as 100 adults and children in all, were complete strangers to my generation. "It was very odd," my cousin Nancy Keating Walsh told me. "I remember all these other people there, and I know they were our cousins, but we didn't mix. They stayed on one side of the hill, and we stayed on the other." That's how I remember it, as well: They ate their fried chicken and potato salad, and we ate ours.

So even though this sprawling family is widely dispersed today, to all corners of the United States and beyond, I hope this book can help bring descendants of the old South Omaha picnickers back together. I'm happy to have talked with a number of these lost cousins during my research, and we have resolved to stay in touch. It may be a cliché, but it also happens to be true: Understanding where we come from helps us understand who we are.

I'VE SPENT MY LIFE as a journalist and writer of nonfiction books. I have always relished the process of deep research—collecting detailed information that I can then use to tell a vivid story, bringing life to my subjects. Verifiable facts, especially names and dates, are a precious commodity in my line of work. Nellie McAuliffe's life story was a long and winding road, and there were more than a few bricks missing as I tried to recreate her journey. Our extended family left few written records of its immigrant experience. If a trove of early family correspondence between Ireland and Omaha exists, I haven't found it. And as is typical of too many American families, we lost entire generations without documenting essential information by asking a simple question of parents and grandparents: Tell me about your life. Unfortunately, even photographs of our immigrant forebears are scarce.

Through American and Irish records, I was able to access remarkable information—the details of Nellie McAuliffe's crossing from Ireland to America by ship, for example. I found another treasure in the Irish Census: an abstract description of the tiny house where Nellie grew up, in the countryside near Limerick. The United States Census, court records, newspaper clippings, and city directories were all invaluable. I leaned heavily on the memories and research of several cousins, and I also gained facts and insights from a two-page Kinnear family history that has been passed around in our family. (Unfortunately, the brief document was not signed, and no one seems to know who wrote it. I believe that it dates to the 1960s.)

Despite these resources, sometimes the most basic biographical information proved to be elusive. Nellie McAuliffe's birthdate is one of many examples. All sources seem to agree that she was born on March 21, but in what year? The Kinnear history says she was born in 1863. But the 1900 U.S. Census suggested a birth year of 1867. Ten years later, the 1910 Census set her birth year as 1865. And at the end of her life, an obituary indicated that she was born in 1862. The Kinnear history also contradicted itself by saying that she had emigrated at age 18 in 1886, which would mean she was born in 1868. In fact, the U.S. government's immigration documentation says that Nellie was 20 years old when she arrived in Boston in July 1883. I believe that confirms her birthdate as March 21, 1863. So a few hours of research later, that missing brick — one of hundreds — had finally, and mercifully, been replaced.

TWO

The Limerick Homeplace

NELLIE MCAULIFFE WAS BORN into a farm family that scratched out a living on a small parcel of land in Murroe, Ireland, a hamlet 15 miles east of Limerick. Her farmer father was Michael McAuliffe. The second-born daughter, she was named after her mother, Ellen (O'Malley) McAuliffe. (Another muddled detail: Various online sources list her mother's maiden name as O'Madey, Madey, or Maley. I found descendants who spell the name O'Malley, so I'm going with that.) On her mother's side, Nellie's people were deeply rooted in little Murroe. Ellen O'Malley was born and raised there, growing up on a small subsistence farm where her parents, Patrick O'Malley and Mary (Devane) O'Malley, both born in 1801, toiled every single day.

Nellie might have seemed destined to follow her mother's path — to marry a local boy and raise children down on the farm, as her older sister, Catherine, had. But she apparently had other ideas, like millions of other Irish during the 19th century. The nation lost nearly half of its population to hunger-driven immigration, dwindling from 8.2 million people in 1840 to 4.4 million by 1910. The surge of immigration began with the Great Famine of the 1840s, caused by a blight that ruined potato crops for several years running, eliminating the primary food source for Ireland's poor. As a result, an Irish diaspora began its spread to English-speaking lands around the globe—across the Irish Sea to Manchester and Liverpool, England, of course, but also to distant destinations, including Australia, New Zealand, Canada, and the United States.

Our Nellie came of age amid another famine that primarily affected her region of western Ireland, beginning in 1879, when she was in her 16th year. What was her life like? Certainly, conveniences would have been scant.

Nellie's family plot was nothing like the vast farms in America's Midwest that we are accustomed to. Even today, many farm fields east of Limerick are carved up by hedges, creeks, and tree rows into plots of perhaps five or ten acres, producing just enough hay to feed a small stable of livestock. Nellie's people were born to that land—and to that way of life. She grew up poor. The farmhouse would have had no electricity; electric lines did not reach such humble rural environs in Ireland until the 1920s and 1930s, long after she had gone. Nor would the family have had indoor plumbing. The toilet would have been a rustic outdoor privy. Water would be hauled from a community well in the vicinity, probably shared with the cluster of seven other small farmhouses identified as neighbors of the McAuliffes in the 1901 Irish Census.

I wasn't able to track Michael McAuliffe's ancestral lineage—not even the names of his parents. He was a poor farmer in an impoverished country, and it seems that government record-keeping of people like McAuliffe was not a priority during his lifetime, which spanned nearly the entirety of the 1800s. A McAuliffe family tree that I found on an ancestry website erroneously suggests that Nellie's Irish-born father, Michael, died in 1893 in Baltimore, Maryland. But the 1901 Irish Census proves that our Michael was alive and living in Murroe eight years later. The confusion is understandable: The Michael McAuliffe who died in Baltimore was also born

CENSUS OF IRELAND, 1901.

(The Examples of the mode of filling up this Table are given on the other side.)

FORM A.

RETURN of the MEMBERS of this FAMILY and their VISITORS, BOARDERS, SERVANTS, &c., who slept or abode in this House on the night of SUNDAY, the 31st of MARCH 1901.

NAME and SURNAME.	RELATION to Head of Family.	RELIGIOUS PROFESSION.	EDUCATION.	AGE.		SEX.	RANK, PROFESSION, OR OCCUPATION.	MARRIAGE.	WHERE BORN.	IRISH LANGUAGE.	
				Males	Females						
Michael McAuliffe	Head	Catholic	Read & write	55		M	Farmer	Married	Co. Limerick	Irish & English	
Ellen McAuliffe	Wife	do.	Read & write		50	F		Married	Co. Limerick	Irish & English	
Georgy McAuliffe	Son	do.	Read & write	20		M	Farmer's Son	Not married	Co. Limerick	Irish & English	

I hereby certify, as required by the Act 63 Vic, cap 6, s 6 (2), that the foregoing Return is correct, according to the best of my knowledge and belief

_____ (Signature of Enumerator.)

I believe the foregoing to be a true Return.

_____ (Signature of Head of Family.)

Nellie McAuliffe's parents and brother in the 1901 Irish Census near Limerick in 1816 — and was also married to a woman named Ellen. As far as I know, they were not related.

The census of 1901 offers an interesting record of how our Michael and Ellen McAuliffe and their children lived. Though the census was taken 18 years after Nellie had departed for America, I am certain the McAuliffes were living in the same place where she had grown up.

The census showed that Nellie's younger brother, Henry, was still living at home as a 30-year-old bachelor. I was surprised by the age difference between her parents: The document said Michael was 85 and Ellen 60. Their oldest child, daughter Catherine, was born in 1858, when Michael would have been 42 and his wife just 17 years old. Michael was identified as a farmer and Henry as a "farmer's son." All three said they were practicing Roman Catholics, and each affirmed that they could read and write, even though a formal education did not become compulsory in Ireland until 1922.

A separate census document gives a fascinating abstract description of the homes of Nellie's parents and their neighbors. Each of the eight homes in the tract was both described and categorized based upon its size and the durability of its building materials. Under this evaluation system, a one-room shack would have been rated as 4th class. The McAuliffe dwelling was just a single notch above that, 3rd class.

The McAuliffes were not renters — Michael owned both the house and the land it stood on. But their home was tiny, with just two rooms. It featured two windows, on the front-facing side. We can deduce that the house was not built to last. The durability scale gave high value to houses built of stone, brick, or concrete and low value to those made of "mud, wood, or other perishable material." The McAuliffe house was rated as perishable. Likewise, roofs of "slate, iron or tiles" had high value, while those of "thatch, wood, or other perishable material" did not. Again, the McAuliffe house was poorly rated. The 3rd-class overall rating came from the sum of the number of rooms (two), the numbers of windows (two), and the numbers assigned based upon building and roofing materials (double zeros) — for a grand total of four.

This rural Murroe census document included seven other properties in the same vicinity. Interestingly, four of those seven homeowners were women — Mary Wren, Johanna Rainsford, Bridget Ryan, and Bridget McCormack. (Perhaps some of their spouses had gone abroad for work?) The male homeowners were our Michael McAuliffe, John Flynn, Patrick Ryan, and Patrick Wren. None owned a mansion; all but one of the homes had four or fewer rooms. But of the eight, Michael and Ellen McAuliffe's little place was the only property with a total rating as low as four. The document also delineated each property's outbuildings, including such things as stables, coach houses, barns, and dairies. Patrick Ryan, who owned the largest house inventoried on the census document, had 11 outbuildings. Johanna Rainsford had four, and several others had three. The McAuliffe property was the only house with a single outbuilding. Perhaps it was a palatial barn, but I doubt it.

I had assumed that our Nellie, like most immigrants of that era, had come from humble circumstances, and the 1901 Irish Census serves as confirmation. In a collection of meager little farmhouses, her homeplace was rated dead last by an official government assessment. She grew up, it seems, in place that was one step up from a mud-and-straw hut.

THREE

The Irish Exodus

NELLIE WAS A FARM GIRL, but the big city of Limerick, then and now Ireland's third largest, was just a short train trip away during her childhood. Limerick straddles the River Shannon, which opens up there into a wide tidal estuary leading to the sea, 40 miles to the west. For centuries, Limerick has been a center for commercial shipping and shipbuilding.

Out in the countryside east of Limerick, the wee train station at the hamlet of Boher was just a mile's walk from Murroe, Nellie's village. From there, she could have been in Limerick's central city in less than an hour. The Kinnear family history suggests that, before she left Ireland, Nellie had a job waiting in Omaha. The document says, "She was offered a job as 'nanny' to a prominent Omahan." Logic suggests that she had worked as a nanny in Ireland, perhaps in Limerick, and made the Omaha connection either in that city or through a relative—a friend, a cousin, an aunt or uncle—who might have emigrated before her. Unfortunately, her precise Omaha connection is another missing brick in the story of her life.

She no doubt would have known many people who left Ireland for the United States. County Limerick, where Murroe is located, and Limerick City must have seemed like ghost towns during Nellie's childhood. For decades, people had been abandoning the region in staggering numbers. In 1841, before the first devastating famine, 162,000 people lived in County Limerick. By the time Nellie was born in 1863, the county's population had declined by more than a third, to 105,000. It had lost another 20,000 by the time Nellie left 20 years later, and then bottomed out at just 72,000 in 1901. County Limerick lost about 90,000 people, well over half of its population, in the 60 years from 1841 to 1901. This calculates to a loss in the county of 125 people every single month over the entirety of those 60 years of the Irish exodus. And while deaths accounted for a portion of the decline, emigration was the primary reason for the steep loss.

Imagine the difficulty, both financially and emotionally, of Nellie's decision to join the legions that left. Every international émigré must show initiative and resolve. Staying put is so much easier. But over the course of human history, emigration for some has become a necessity, not an option. I believe that was the case with our Nellie. Considering the prospects at home, leaving became an inevitability, even though she must have known that she would be seeing her mother and father for the final time as she turned her back on Limerick.

There is a yin and yang to these decisions—a dark side that is inextricably entangled with a light side. As Milan Kundera, the Czech writer who lived in exile in France after escaping the Communist regime of Czechoslovakia in the 1970s, wrote in his novel *Ignorance*, "Anyone who decides to leave his country forever has to resign himself never to see his family again." But sometimes there is no choice. This is the opening stanza of "Home," a poem by Warsan Shire, a contemporary writer whose family fled the despair in their native Somalia:

no one leaves home unless
home is the mouth of a shark
you only run for the border
when you see the whole city running as well

Metaphorically speaking, Nellie McAuliffe joined nearly half the population of Ireland in sprinting toward the border in the second half of the 1800s. She said her goodbyes in late June of 1883, a few days after the Summer Solstice. She left clutching a ticket on a steamship that would take her to America. Her trip began in Limerick, where she boarded a train for Cork, 65 miles due south. Just beyond Cork was the port city of Queenstown, Ireland (later renamed Cobh), a final European stop for passenger ships bound for the United States and Canada. (Three decades later, Queenstown was the final port of call for the Titanic's doomed ocean crossing.)

Nellie was ticketed for a steerage berth on the SS *Pavonia*, a Cunard Line passenger ship based in Liverpool, England. Built in Glasgow, Scotland, the *Pavonia* was a 430-foot, coal-fired steam ship, with triple masts for auxiliary sails. The *Pavonia* was still nearly new when Nellie boarded for her passage on Wednesday, June 27, 1883. It was just the ship's fifth Atlantic crossing, according to its records; it would go on to become a workhorse for Cunard, with 83 round-trips voyages — nearly all from Liverpool to Boston and back, with stops in Queenstown, Ireland. In her 17 years of service, the *Pavonia* delivered more than 50,000 people like Nellie McAuliffe to America.

The ship could accommodate about 1,700 passengers — 200 in first- or second-class, and the rest in steerage, the cheapest form of travel. According to a passenger manifest that I found, only 460 men, women, and children were traveling in steerage during Nellie's crossing, which made her trip less taxing than for many who crossed the ocean below-deck.

Nellie McAuliffe was born in Murroe, Ireland,
and William Kinnear near Fyvie, Scotland

Nellie paid the equivalent of about $30 for her ticket on the *Pavonia*, a small fortune at a time when a young Irishwoman might have been lucky to earn a dime a day as a maid. And what did she get for her money? Basic meals were provided, but unlike those traveling

The SS *Pavonia* (PAVONIA PHOTOS BY NORWEGIAN HERITAGE)

on the more expensive tickets, steerage passengers were not guaranteed a specific space onboard, let alone a room. They were packed like sardines in dark chambers in the windowless bowels of the ship. Prime sections on deck were reserved for the higher classes, so steerage passengers who wanted fresh air huddled downwind of the belching black coal exhaust. Viruses and other communicable ailments swept through the steerage hovels, and deaths on board were common. "For most immigrants . . . the experience of steerage was like a nightmare," according to one account I found. "The conditions were so crowded, so dismally dark, so unsanitary, and so foul-smelling."

Some years after Nellie's journey, the continuing mistreatment of steerage-class passengers prompted President William Howard Taft to demand an investigation by the U.S. Immigration Commission. Its report offered a grim portrait:

The open deck space reserved for steerage passengers is usually very limited, and situated in the worst part of the ship, subject to the most violent motion, to the dirt from the stacks and the odors from the hold and

Travelers onboard the SS *Pavonia*

galleys. . . . The only provisions for eating are frequently shelves or benches along the sides or in the passages of sleeping compartments. Dining rooms are rare and, if found, are often shared with berths installed along the walls. Toilets and washrooms are completely inadequate . . .

The ventilation is almost always inadequate, and the air soon becomes foul. The unattended vomit of the seasick, the odors of none-too-clean bodies, the reek of food and the awful stench of the nearby toilet rooms make the atmosphere of steerage such that it is a marvel that human flesh can endure it. . . . Most immigrants lie in their berths for most of the voyage, in a stupor caused by the foul air. The food often repels them. . . . It is almost impossible to keep personally clean. All of these conditions are naturally aggravated by the crowding.

FORTUNATELY, NELLIE'S TIME in this hellscape was relatively brief. Atlantic crossings by sail often took six weeks or more, but beginning in the 1850s, steam power had drastically reduced the duration—typically, to 15 days or so. Records show that the *Pavonia* docked in Boston on Saturday, July 7. Remarkably, on a crossing that spanned 2,600 nautical miles, Nellie had spent just 10 nights as a steerage sardine.

I was able to locate Nellie McAuliffe on an archival copy of the *Pavonia's* manifest for her crossing. Her page of steerage passengers reads like the membership roster of St. Mary's Cathedral in Limerick. Nearly everyone had Irish surnames—McFadden, Maguire, O'Connell, Casey, Burke, Leary, Sullivan, Carney, Callahan, Driscoll, Sheehan, Leahy, and more. They were identified by name, age, occupation, and intended destination. It was a working-class group—servants, laborers, shepherds, weavers, farmers. Our Nellie was listed as steerage passenger Number 359. The brief Kinnear family history has just a few sentences about Nellie's emigration, including this one: "She left Ireland and sailed to America with her Brother Jack and friend Bridget Murphy." The next passenger in line behind Nellie, Number 360, was a 16-year-old Irish girl named Bridget, but her surname was not listed as Murphy. On the manifest, her last name was long and indecipherable, beginning with a C. But is seems likely that the Bridget standing behind Nellie as they exited the ship was the same girl referenced in the family history. Each had two pieces of baggage and were identified as servants. They may have had another female companion. A third young woman, Ellen O'Neil, was grouped with Nellie and Bridget on the manifest. O'Neil was Irish and 18 years old, and her occupation was recorded as "spinster" — meaning a weaver of cloth, not an unmarried older woman. All three young women were said to be initially destined for Massachusetts. But in the standard phrasing on the ship manifest, Nellie and the other itinerant travelers were described as "intending (a) protracted sojourn." Nebraska was not noted as her destination. But isn't that a rather poetic description of what she faced in America — a protracted sojourn, wending, bobbing, and weaving her way through life?

One other detail from the manifest: There was no sign of the "Brother Jack" whom the Kinnear family document suggested was Nellie's traveling mate. I have been able to confirm that Nellie had only two siblings, both of whom stayed in Ireland. Her older sister, Catherine McAuliffe Nicholas, born in 1858, raised eight children as a farm wife not far from the McAuliffe homestead in Murroe. She died there in 1913, in her mid-50s. Nellie also had a younger brother, Henry, born in 1871 — the bachelor "farmer's son" listed on the 1901 Irish Census. There was no other McAuliffe aboard the *Pavonia* with Nellie, and I have found no record of a brother Jack McAuliffe in Ireland or the United States.

Nellie was not quite home free when she exited the ship: She had to face the gauntlet of immigrant screening in Boston. Every traveler in that era had heard horror stories of prospective immigrants who were deemed unfit, returned to the ship, and summarily deported. Nellie arrived while the U.S. was in the midst of a transitional period of immigration policy. In the 1870s, the U.S. Supreme Court had declared the oversight of immigration to be a federal responsibility. Beginning in 1893, the federal government would begin more systematic screening that included a 31-point biographical questionnaire; a minimum of $25 in cash in hand; and exclusion of convicts, polygamists, anarchists, and those with "a loathsome or a dangerous contagious disease," including such things as tuberculosis, venereal disease, and obvious bacterial infections of the eyes and skin.

Ellen (Nellie) McAuliffe, SS *Pavonia* passenger No. 359

But when Nellie arrived in 1883, individual states had continued to enforce immigration rules — and there weren't many. Federal officials collected a 50-cent "head tax" and scanned arrivals to screen out Asians under the Chinese Exclusion Act of 1882, through which Congress banned immigration by Chinese laborers. The same immigration laws excluded "idiots, lunatics, convicts" and anyone who seemed unable to support themselves. Before boarding the

```
Name  McAuliffe, Ellen              Age  20    Sex  F
        (Port  Boston
Arrived (Date  July 7, 1883        S.S.  "Pavonia"

If in U.S. before  No               Occupation  Servant

Birthplace (Nationality)  Ireland

Country of which citizen   ---

Last residence            Ireland

Destination (State of which U.S.
intend to become inhabitant)

Mental and bodily condition   ---   List No. 359

                                          Jd
```

Nellie McAuliffe's immigration card

Pavonia in Ireland, Nellie would have undergone a cursory physical examination—by a doctor or nurse employed by the Cunard Lines who had a motivation to find her fit.

Our Nellie passed the idiot test in Boston. A government immigration card with rudimentary information about Nellie on the day of her arrival showed three dashes (- - -) beside the heading "Mental and Bodily Condition." That line on the card referenced her *Pavonia* passenger number—"List No. 359"—and was initialed by "jd." This suggests that some random agent at the dock—John Doe?—looked her over and was satisfied that she was fit enough to enter the United States of America. Soon, our ancestor found herself enroute to the final destination of her 4,000-mile "protracted sojourn": South Omaha, Nebraska.

FOUR

A Booming Cowtown

NELLIE MCAULIFFE MADE HER WAY west across America via the transcontinental railroad, which had opened coast to coast in 1869. Seven separate railroads funneled people and products from the eastern half of the United States into the busy railyard in Council Bluffs, Iowa, Omaha's twin city on the Missouri River. (From there, any trip farther west on the railroad mainlines would have been via the mighty Union Pacific.) Nellie's train journey would have taken just three or four days, with stops in big cities and small towns along the way every hour or two. It surely seemed a luxurious mode of travel after her time in steamship steerage purgatory.

Imagine the wonders she must have seen crossing half of the country, peering through the glass as the train clicked along at 20 miles per hour. The sheer size of her adopted home country surely made her wide-eyed. Her homeland is just 300 miles long and 170 miles wide. Two Irelands would fit inside the borders of Nebraska alone.

Nellie arrived in Omaha at an opportune time. Twenty years earlier, the city was a dusty outpost on the edge of the western prairie, with a population of barely 1,500 people. But the Nebraska Territory had gained state status in 1867, and that brought a surge in both population and agricultural investment. Together with Council Bluffs, Omaha had become a major rail hub, and the comings-and-goings of all those trains induced the growth of an industry that would define Omaha for several generations.

Then as now, ranching was big business in that region, where wide-open spaces were perfect for grazing livestock (as it was for the slaughtered buffalo that sheep and cattle had replaced). But the supply chain linking meat with meat-eaters was flawed. In the late 1870s, Omaha had a modestly sized livestock yard and a few small meatpackers just south of its downtown business district. The Union Pacific junction in Omaha-Council Bluffs offered easy access for incoming loads of cattle, lambs, and hogs from the west and outgoing butchered meat heading toward eastern big cities in ice-cooled trains cars via the UP bridge over the Missouri River, completed in 1872. But ranchers needed a much bigger livestock yard and high-volume butchering plants. The supply of animals was good, and so was demand for the meat. But the processing of standing livestock into the end product was a crimp in the system.

With investment and encouragement by railroaders, ranchers, and bankers, graders and earth-movers in the early 1880s began smoothing the terrain in a swath of sloped farmland six miles south of downtown Omaha, near what is now 30th and Q Streets in South Omaha, then a separate city. South O's Union Stockyards was founded in 1883, the year of Nellie's arrival in America. It would quickly become one of the world's largest livestock-processing centers. Meatpacking plants and related specialty businesses sprouted like mushrooms around the Stockyards, and thousands of American migrants and European immigrants streamed toward Omaha to grab the abundant packinghouse jobs. Overnight, Omaha became a booming cowtown, its population increasing from 30,000 in 1880 to 140,000 just ten years later.

THIS WOULD BE A GOOD PLACE to tell the backstory of why Nellie chose Omaha. Alas, I don't know — another missing brick, and another example of how the most basic (and, often, important) details of a family's history can get lost in a single generation. My grandmother, Nellie's daughter Eileen, would likely have known. Eileen's children, my mother and her four siblings, might also have known why Nellie ended up in Omaha, beyond the lore about a promised nannying job. But they are all gone — and, sadly, so is Nellie's Omaha origin story.

Of course, the Irish famine diaspora had sprinkled Irish men and women all around the English-speaking world. More than a few of those emigres ended up in South Omaha, in a neighborhood near the Stockyards that became known as Irish Hill. Perhaps Nellie was related to one of them. Or maybe the connection came through her friend and emigration companion Bridget Murphy. Records show that Bridget was born near Wexford, Ireland, 110 miles from Limerick, on the opposite side of the country. She was the sixth of eight children born to Thomas and Catherine Murphy. I am not sure how the two teenagers became acquainted in the Old Country, since they were born and raised far apart. But I do know for certain that the bond they made in Ireland endured for more than a half-century in South Omaha. According to the Kinnear family history:

"Ellen [Nellie] and Bridget remained friends. Bridget was bridesmaid for them [Nellie and her future husband] and later married Patrick A. Furlong. Bridget owned a boarding house where Ellen's daughters, Grace and Eileen, worked from time to and listened to her stories about Ireland."

Marriage and daughters? That's getting ahead of our story. First, we have to meet the groom-to-be. For that, we travel back to the United Kingdom.

FIVE

The Kinnears of Scotland

NELLIE MCAULIFFE'S FUTURE HUSBAND was born some 500 miles from her hometown in Ireland, across the Irish Sea and far north to a remote, beautiful, and rather forbidding corner of northeastern Scotland. His name was William Kinnear, and his ancestors had deep roots in a tiny baronial village called Fyvie, a name thought to be drawn from the Gaelic words for Deer Hill. The village is located just 20 miles inland from the often-blustery North Sea. *(See the UK map on page 16.)* Fyvie is 25 miles north of the region's largest city, Aberdeen, a port town known today for its Scotch whiskey distilleries and as a center of the United Kingdom's offshore oil industry.

Fyvie hasn't changed much in the 150-plus years since William Kinnear began his life. Today, it is still a collection of a few dozen tightly clustered stone houses surrounded by farm fields. The village is 50 miles northeast of the Cairngorms, one of the rugged mountain ranges that give the Scottish Highlands its name. By the time it reaches Fyvie, the mountainous topography flattens into hills that gently slope toward the sea, which provides the region with a chilly oceanic climate year 'round. Visitors there are advised to bring sweaters and raingear. On average, it rains two out of every five days. Summertime high temperatures typically peak in the mid-60s, and lows are consistently near freezing for seven months of the year. But as much as its North Sea–influenced weather, Fyvie's latitude defines the rhythms of life there. It is located just north of the 57th parallel, comparable to northern Quebec, Canada. At the Summer Solstice, Fyvie enjoys 18 hours of sunlight, with sunset after 10 P.M. and sunrise six hours later, just after 4 A.M. Conversely, at the December Winter Solstice, the sun sets at 3:30 P.M. and does not rise again for nearly 18 hours, just before 9 A.M.

Despite the cold, the rain, and the interminable winter darkness, human beings have occupied that place for some 15,000 years, dating to the end of the Paleolithic age. Those ancient inhabitants left behind a relic—a stone megalith that stands 7 feet high, located three miles north of Fyvie at the summit of Monk's Hill. Archeologists say there were more stones at the site in the early 19th century, but some were repurposed for use in the foundations of local buildings. (You have to appreciate the famous Scottish ingenuity—and frugality.) Experts suppose that the megaliths were part of a circle of stones, similar to other late-Paleolithic monuments scattered across Scotland and elsewhere in the United Kingdom—most famously at Stonehenge, in the south of England. A short hike away from Monk's Hill, there are traces of an old Roman road dating to invasions nearly 2,000 years ago. It's not much of a stretch to imagine that Caesar's boys stood gawking at the Fyvie rocks.

The Monk's Hill stone is one of two local attractions. For more than 800 years, Fyvie has been known primarily for the other one: Fyvie Castle, a gigantic royal fortress believed to have been originally built in the 12th Century under orders of William the Lion, the long-reigning King of Scots. Over the centuries, the castle was expanded and improved as it was passed from one member of the Scottish and English gentry to another—families with surnames such as Lindsay, Preston, Seton, and Gordon. The final private owner was Alexander Leith, a Scotsman who was born lucky. He

Fyvie Castle in Scotland

was raised in Aberdeen by a wealthy family that had enjoyed several generations of peerage status — Baron This and Baroness That. After a European education and a stint in the Royal Navy, Leith sailed for the United States, where he had a second stroke of luck. While in Missouri in 1871, Leith met, courted, and married a young American woman named Marie Louise January, whose father was one of the most successful businessmen in booming St. Louis. Derick January had financial stakes in a wide array of industries — wholesale groceries, banking, insurance, hotels, and metal manufacturing. He guided his new son-in-law toward a career in America's burgeoning steel industry, and young Leith was soon the owner of a Chicago-area firm that would eventually become U.S. Steel, the world's first billion-dollar corporation. Leith was set for life. In 1889, at just 42 years old, he retired and returned to his homeland, where he purchased and restored Fyvie Castle, living out his final three decades in luxury as 1st Baron Leith of Fyvie. The National Trust for Scotland bought the property in 1984 and opened it for public tours.

No, you will not find the name of our ancestor William Kinnear in the long trail of ownership of Fyvie Castle. More likely, Kinnear and his people would have been found on the castle grounds toiling with hoes, rakes, and pitchforks. For centuries, Fyvie Castle was an economic focal point of that locale. Then as now, the village had fewer than 500 people, and many of the residents would have earned a living, however meager, by working for the castle gentry in one trade or another. I have traced a line of our Scottish Kinnears back to the late 1600s, and many were born, lived, and died in rural villages within a few miles of the castle — walking distance for the servant class. As with our Irish ancestors from rural Limerick, many of our Scottish ancestors were farmers, as well, with a few skilled tradesmen scattered in, including a master tailor, a blacksmith, and a saddle-maker in the 1800s.

I WAS HAPPY TO LEARN that our Scottish ancestor came from a place with two distinct antiquities that have changed little over the centuries. Just imagine: His descendants can visit both of them — and stare with awe (at the castle) and puzzlement (at the megalith), in the same way that our William Kinnear surely did when he was young.

William was born in Rayne, Scotland, south of Fyvie, an only child and the namesake of his father. For that era, William's parents were unusually old at the time of his birth. William Sr. was 30, and his wife, Elizabeth Horn Kinnear, was even older, at 34. William Sr. led an itinerant life compared with most of his kin — in that he was born, lived, and died in at least three different places. He was born on September 13, 1827, in Fordoun, Scotland, near the North Sea coast 50 miles south of Fyvie. In 1851, a Scottish census found William Sr. living in Aberlemno, 25 miles south of his birthplace. At age 24, he had taken on an interesting trade, as an apprentice saddle-maker. Within five years, William had moved north to Rayne, perhaps to ply his leather trade. It was there that Kinnear met and married Elizabeth, who gave birth to their son, my maternal great-grandfather William, on December 29, 1860.

Going back a generation further, I found another William Kinnear—our ancestor's grandfather. He was a lifelong resident of the Fordoun area, born there in 1797. He worked as a "master tailor," according to an old Scottish census. His wife, Jean Stuart Kinnear, was born in 1799 in Kincardineshire County, not far from her husband's hometown. Like William and Elizabeth, it appears that William and Jean Kinnear also had a single child that they named William.

Records do not reveal the precise date that our William Kinnear's father died. But his mother, Elizabeth Horn Kinnear, lived a long life, dying in her hometown of Rayne in 1907, at age 84. It must have been difficult for her when our William, her only child, emigrated to the United States in about 1890, as she was entering her dotage. But Elizabeth had many cousins and other relatives nearby to keep her company. Her family had been living in Fyvie for five or six generations, dating to the late 1600s.

You can consult my version of William Kinnear's family tree on page 33 for an overview of his pure-Scottish genealogy, but here are a few highlights of his maternal ancestors:

- His mother's father, George Horn (1788-1869), was a lifelong Fyvien. So were George's parents, Adan William Horn, a master blacksmith who lived from 1752 to 1840, and Sarah Milne Horn (1753-1825). Adan Horn's father was Alexander Horn (1712-1793).
- William's maternal grandmother, Elspeth Hatt Horn (1794-1844) was yet another lifelong Fyvien. Her father was William Hatt, born in 1759. He was the son of James Hatt,

born in 1712. William Hatt died young, at age 43 in 1802, after fathering Elspeth and five other children. His death left his wife, Elspeth Taylor Hatt, age 38 at the time, with six children to raise, the oldest 12 and the youngest just 2. She must have been a strong woman; she lived a long life, dying at 79 in 1844, four decades after her husband

- ·Even further back on that ancestral line, I found that Elspeth Taylor Hatt's parents were George Andrew Taylor (born 1735) and Jean Gib Taylor (born May 9, 1714). Jean Taylor's parents were William Gib and Margaret Forest, both born in northeastern Scotland in roughly 1690 — 4,000 miles and several centuries removed from their descendant's life in South Omaha.

Despite the distance in time and space, traces of the ancestral DNA of these seemingly remote Scottish relatives — Horns, Hatts, Taylors, Gibs, and the rest — still course through our veins today.

Like Ireland, Scotland experienced a steep population decline during the 19th Century. Experts estimate that a million Scottish men, women, and children left for the United States. By and large, they came for economic opportunity, although each immigrant's circumstances and reasons for leaving home surely is unique. Some were the children of peasant farmers who eked out a livelihood on rented farmsteads so small that they could walk the circumference in 10 or 15 minutes. These tiny plots could not support another family, so children were expected to strike out on their own. Like Nellie McAuliffe in Ireland, many of these young people emigrated in their late teenage years, as soon as they came of age, to Australia and New Zealand, Canada and America.

But our William Kinnear had a rather unorthodox immigrant story in that he left home sometime just short of his 30th birthday. Many who emigrated at that advanced age did so with their families — a

William Kinnear's Family Tree

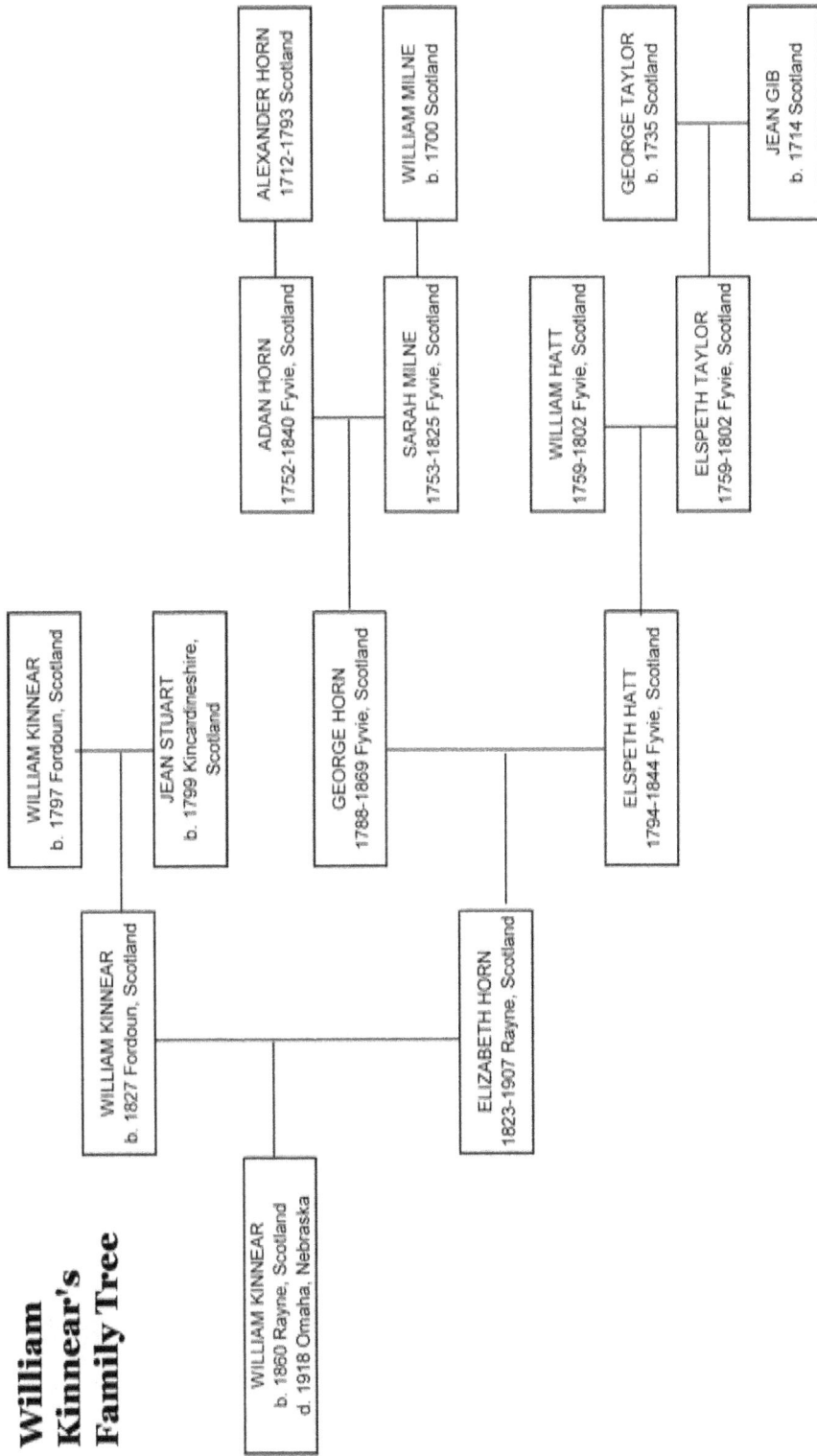

WILLIAM KINNEAR
b. 1797 Fordoun, Scotland

JEAN STUART
b. 1799 Kincardineshire, Scotland

WILLIAM KINNEAR
b. 1827 Fordoun, Scotland

WILLIAM KINNEAR
b. 1860 Rayne, Scotland
d. 1918 Omaha, Nebraska

ELIZABETH HORN
1823-1907 Rayne, Scotland

GEORGE HORN
1788-1869 Fyvie, Scotland

ELSPETH HATT
1794-1844 Fyvie, Scotland

ADAN HORN
1752-1840 Fyvie, Scotland

SARAH MILNE
1753-1825 Fyvie, Scotland

WILLIAM HATT
1759-1802 Fyvie, Scotland

ELSPETH TAYLOR
1759-1802 Fyvie, Scotland

ALEXANDER HORN
1712-1793 Scotland

WILLIAM MILNE
b. 1700 Scotland

GEORGE TAYLOR
b. 1735 Scotland

JEAN GIB
b. 1714 Scotland

spouse, children, perhaps even parents. But William apparently left on his own, leaving behind his aging mother, Elizabeth. There are discrepancies about the precise year of his emigration. Whenever he said his goodbyes, William had had to resign himself to the fact that he would never see his mother again, part of the yin and yang of the immigration process.

SIX

Home to South Omaha

AS WITH NELLIE MCAULIFFE, I don't know for certain why our Bill Kinnear left his native country, but I can make a couple of informed guesses. As an only child, William would have stood to inherit any real estate and personal property that his parents happened to own — land, a house, livestock. His immigration in full adulthood suggests that there was no family property to inherit, and I found evidence of that in several Scottish censuses during the late 1800s. In each, Kinnear's father was identified as a simple agricultural laborer, not a landowner.

The censuses of 1871 and 1881 said the Kinnears lived in a rural tract known as Dovehills. I was not able to find a description of their home, but I did locate an historical document from the 1880s that included a detailed survey of that region's farms. Like much of northern Scotland, the Rayne/Fyvie area once was dotted with peat moss bogs. Farmhands like the Kinnears would be hired to cut out blocks of peat, which was then dried to a brick-like consistency and used like firewood to heat homes or as cookstove fuel. A precious commodity for thousands of years, the local moss supply was dwindling fast and was being replaced by cultivated fields of grain or vegetables, according to the *Ordnance Gazetteer of Scotland*'s analysis in about 1885. It reported, "The peat is being gradually exhausted, and at no distant time the ground will doubtless become ploughed land." The same document offered a glimpse of the living conditions of "crofters and cottars," the lowly farmers of northern Scotland who paid rent to landowners to lease plots of land. Cottars were legally defined as "a peasant occupying a cottage and land of not more than half an acre at a rent of not more than five pounds a year." Crofters generally worked larger plots, of up to a dozen acres or so. Both forms of tenants lived in small, thatched-roof dwellings constructed of fieldstone. The document's assessment of the state of farming in the region made a clear differentiation between the wellbeing of the landowners and their tenants:

Agriculture is in an advanced state, and is carried on by an intelligent, industrious, and well-behaved people. The farms are all of moderate size, with a considerable number of crofts. The farmhouses and steadings on the larger holdings are generally good, but the crofters' and cottars' houses are in some districts very indifferent, and sorely need improvement.

I reckon that our Kinnear ancestors resided in one of those "indifferent" domiciles.

BEYOND FAMILY FINANCES, Bill's age and his solo journey from Scotland might offer further clues to his emigration motivation. He grew up in a sparsely populated rural area where he would have been directly related to many of his neighbors on his mother's side of the family. The fact that he was still single as he approached 30 suggests that opportunities for romance in Fyvie were limited.

Perhaps he set out on his own "protracted sojourn" with a goal of finding a wife. I do know that, whether by design or by coincidence, his marital status changed very soon when he reached his destination in Nebraska.

Some records, including the Kinnear family history and the 1900 federal census, say that he crossed the Atlantic and arrived in America in 1890. I was not able to find his name in immigration records or steamship passenger manifests—another missing brick. One genealogical chart put together by our distant relatives in Scotland says our Bill emigrated in 1890 but did not reach Omaha until the fall of 1892. But I discovered that Bill Kinnear was in Omaha by 1890. That year's R.L. Polk City Directory for Omaha showed him living as a boarder at 1907 North 24th Street, near Grace Street. He was employed as a "stationary engineer"—a furnace or boiler maintenance man—at the Paxton Building downtown. That is the trade that our ancestor plied for years to come, so I am certain this was my great-grandfather. I also know with certainty that he was still in Omaha in the spring of 1892. On April 2 that year, he stood before a federal district court clerk in Omaha and declared his intention to become a U.S. citizen, *"and to renounce and abjure forever all allegiance and fidelity to all and any foreign Price, Potentate, State and sovereignty whatever, and particularly to Queen of Great Britain of whom I was a subject."*

Pathfinding emigrants often are followed by kin from back home, and I suspect that our Bill Kinnear had a family connection that drew him to Omaha: a man named Walter F. Kinnear. Born in Scotland on August 5, 1855, Walter arrived in Omaha in about 1875 and applied for naturalized citizenship there in 1888, four years before Bill. In 1890, when William showed up in the local city directory as a boiler-tender, Walter Kinnear was listed in the same directory as a gunsmith and traveling salesman for Omaha's Collins Gun Company. Walter was living on Florence Boulevard in north

Omaha, just five or six blocks from Bill. Their proximity seems like more than coincidence. Born five years apart, I suspect they were cousins. Walter Kinnear went on to have a long career in the firearms business, including as proprietor of the Omaha Gun Company. He and his wife, Dora, had several children, including daughters Edith,

(Above and on next page) Walter and William Kinnear citizenship documents, four years apart

Mabel, and Clara. Walter lived out his life in the Florence area and was buried there, at Forest Lawn Memorial Park, after his death on June 2, 1924.

The United States Census, taken every 10 years since 1790, is a wonderful resource for those doing this sort of family research. The census of 1890 would offer a font of information about the early years in Omaha of Bill Kinnear and Nellie McAuliffe. The first census taken after their arrival in the US, the 1890 edition likely would reveal where Nellie was living and how she was employed. Was she, for example, a live-in nanny for a "prominent Omahan," as the Kinnear family history suggested? Likewise, the 1890 census would reveal key details about Bill's first years in America, including confirmation of the Omaha city directory's information about where he lived and worked. But the notorious 1890 census has left a blank spot in this and countless other genealogical explorations. In 1921, a fire in the basement at the U.S. Department of Commerce building in Washington, D.C., left the original — and only — copy of the 1890 census badly damaged by fire, smoke, and water. A decade later, amid the dire economy of the Great Depression, the federal government made the horrible decision to destroy the damaged records rather than save them for future restoration. "This is a genuine tragedy of records," the Virginia-based historian Kellee Blake has written, "and eternally anguishing to researchers."

Count me among the eternally anguished.

Lacking information from the 1890 census, I was unable to unearth anything about Nellie's first 10 years in Omaha, from the summer of 1883, when she presumably arrived, until 1893. Nellie's name does not show up in any of the annual city directories published during her early years in Omaha. Likewise, I have meager information about Bill Kinnear's early days in Nebraska, beyond what I found in the 1890 Omaha directory.

But I do know exactly what Bill and Nellie were doing on a particular winter's day in 1893: gazing into one another's eyes and saying "I do." They were married on January 22, 1893. That was a Monday, so it surely was a modest ceremony, not one of the big South Omaha events to which their heirs would become accustomed. Nellie's old Irish friend, Bridget Murphy, served as bridesmaid. By that date, Bridget was married herself and the mother of an infant son — the first of nine children she would bear. In 1891, she had wed Walter Furlong, a South Omaha Stockyards laborer and the Iowa-born son of Irish immigrants.

Both Nellie and Bill had waited a long time to marry and procreate. In 1900, the median age for a woman's first marriage and childbirth in the United States was about 22. (Today, the average for both is about 27.) Nellie was 29 and Bill 32 when they married, and the newlyweds got busy right away building a family. Their first child was born in November 1893, 10 months after the wedding. Following a three-generation Kinnear tradition, he was named William, after his father. Nellie was four months shy of her 31st birthday when her first baby was born, and she would be occupied by pregnancy and childbirth for the entirety of her 30s. If it's true that she had spent her 20s working as a nanny in Omaha, then she put that training to good use in her own life.

Her second child, a daughter named Grace, arrived 22 months after Bill Jr., in September 1895. Next came my grandmother, Eileen, born in February 1897, 17 months after Grace. A second son, Harry, arrived in June 1899. Daughter Clara arrived in 1901, and the final child of Bill and Nellie Kinnear was a son named Robert. He was born on December 1, 1902, when Nellie was 39 years old. The family was complete—and symmetrical: a husband, a wife, three boys, three girls.

AS THE FAMILY HAD EXPANDED, so did South Omaha, driven by the economic engine of the Stockyards. Each day, roughly 20,000 animals would arrive to be slaughtered, butchered, packaged, and shipped out, typically by trains bound for eastern cities. Armour and the other big packinghouses, linked by chutes to the Stockyards, were always desperate for butchers and laborers to process all that beef, lamb, and pork. And just as proximity to the yards was essential to the meatpackers, the firms preferred that employees live nearby — close enough to hear the screaming whistles that summoned them to work each morning. To that end, Armour and the rest encouraged real estate development in the meatpacking district, and soon new neighborhoods of modest little houses were sprouting all over the hilly terrain surrounding the Stockyards and its pens of bellowing cattle, squealing hogs, and bleating sheep.

One such neighborhood just south of Q Street, the busy east-west main road, was known as Jetter's Addition, after a German immigrant named Balthas Jetter. His surname was often on the lips of South Omahans: Jetter owned a sprawling brewery at 30th and Y Streets, and his brands — Jetter's Bock, Gold Top, and Old Age — were favorites among early meatpackers.

In part to house his brewery employees, Jetter had a hand in development of hundreds of homes on land immediately south of the Stockyards. Many were simple, cheap houses of just two or three rooms thrown up quickly on tiny lots 60 feet wide by 150 feet deep,

Jetter Brewery, South 30th Street, South Omaha

one-fifth of an acre. Some were so tightly spaced that neighbors could nearly shake hands out their side windows. In January 1899, an advertisement in the *Omaha Bee* offered three-room houses in Jetter's Addition for $750, including the tiny lot.

Our Bill Kinnear had a better idea: DIY. He and Nellie purchased a pair of adjoining lots, numbers 12 and 13 on Block 6 of Jetter's Addition, and built homes on both of them. The lots, one much larger than the norm, totaled nearly a full acre, and most of it was good flat land elevated 10 feet above S Street, just west of 30th Street, barely a five-minute walk from several packinghouses. To boot, they were just two blocks away from the home of Nellie's best friend, Bridget Murphy Furlong.

Records are sketchy about the precise date of the Kinnear homestead's construction. Modern real estate records say both structures were built in 1900. But my research suggests that Bill had built a small, single-story house at what is now 3010 S Street by 1896, shortly after he and Nellie's second child was born. A city directory showed him living at that address in 1896. He then began building a larger, two-story place next door, at 3014 S Street, where they were living by 1900.

According to family lore, Bill Kinnear, short of stature but stout as cast iron, built both houses with his own two calloused hands, working nights and Sunday for most of five years. He hauled by wheelbarrow every stone used to set up the cellars, as the story goes, then did the framing, carpentry, plumbing, roofing, and finish work. When the larger house became habitable, they moved their clothing and furnishings from the smaller place next door, then rented out that house. The larger Kinnear home stood out among the tiny, cookie-cutter houses found in much of the neighborhood. It had four small bedrooms, a living room, dining room, kitchen, and bathroom. A garage, shed, and large garden were added in the backyard. For four generations, into the 1960s, that house would serve as the gravitational center of the Kinnear family and descendants.

Consumed by baby-raising and home-building, Bill and Nellie Kinnear did not take time to document their life in photographs. Posed studio photography probably seemed like an expensive luxury to these frugal immigrants, although a cheaper alternative had arrived in the 1890s with the invention of the Kodak Brownie camera. I reached out to a number of my cousins to check their family archives for old Kinnear photos. Most struck out. But my Omaha Dundis cousins (our mothers were sisters) struck gold. These five sisters—Judy Robak, Mary Lincoln, Barb Weishapl, Susan Pral, and Terri Ellis—searched their files and found a torn and faded picture of two women in modest clothing on a porch with three children. On the back, someone had written "House where Grandma Strack was born," referring to Eileen Kinnear Strack, the five sisters' grandmother and Bill and Nellie's daughter. I believe it shows the house at 3010 S Street, the smaller and first of the two built by Bill Kinnear. There are no identifications of the figures on the porch, unfortunately. The woman on the left, holding a baby in her lap, has the black hair, rather long face, and square jawline common in the Kinnear line. But I believe that the older-looking woman standing on the right is Nellie. She, too, is dark-haired and long-faced with a prominent jaw. If the photo was taken in late 1897, the two children at the standing woman's feet could be Nellie's son Billy, born in 1893, and daughter Grace, born in 1895. The infant might be Eileen, born in February 1897. Nellie might well have been pregnant with her fourth child. I don't know for certain, but the seated woman, who seems a few years younger than the other, could be Nellie's old Irish friend Bridget Furlong, who lived nearby. While the identifications are only my best guesses, it was a miracle that the Dundis girls found this precious photograph—the only one of Nellie, as far as I know.

It was a short walk from the Kinnear home to any of the hulking, red brick factories of the Big Five firms—Armour, Swift, Dold/Wilson, Cudahy, and Morris—that had begun to nationalize

This photo appears to show Nellie McAuliffe Kinnear (right) in about 1898 at the first of two houses built by her husband on S Street in South Omaha. The children on the right probably are Billy and Grace Kinnear, her oldest. The woman on the left might be Nellie's Irish friend Bridget Murphy Furlong. The baby could be one of Bridget's—she had nine children. Or it could be Eileen, my grandmother, Nellie's third child.

meat production in America. Inside, workers slaughtered, butchered, packaged, and distributed cattle, hogs, and lambs brought to market at the Stockyards. The livestock yards and packinghouses defined South Omaha for five generations, from the 1880s to the 1960s. Bob and Nellie Kinnear would live out their lives within sniffing distance of the slaughterhouses. That was

South Omaha—blood and toil, stinky and sweaty. There were no mansions in this corner of town. It was and is a blue-collar place whose lifeblood flows from an ever-changing stream of immigrants—once from Europe, now from Latin America and Africa.

South Omaha's founders made it easy for newcomers to navigate. There are few of the winding boulevards and broad avenues that you find in wealthier sections of Omaha. No, South Omaha was designed by a draftsman's ruler, not an artist's brush. That quadrant of the city is laid out in a sensible grid between the Missouri River to the east, 72nd Street to the west, Vinton and Grover Streets to the north, and Harrison Street to the south. Even the street names are user-friendly—ascending numbers from east to west, the ascending alphabet and a handful of presidents' names from north to south. Many neighborhoods were Balkanized by ethnicity, with Catholic church steeples as beacons for each nationality. Whatever your native European language, you could find someone to talk to in South Omaha.

Meatpackers were beckoned to work by rooftop whistles that roused them from bed six mornings a week, then blew periodic blasts as clock-in time approached. It was physically demanding, assembly-line work—on your feet, repeating the same task over and over until the whistle blew at day's end. Many laborers then retreated to the beer joints that lined Q Street, the meatpacking district's main drag. These saloons catered to two distinct clienteles. Thirsty out-of-town farmers and ranchers toted heavy wallets into the barrooms after bringing their livestock to market. They sat on stools beside the blood-stained, accented immigrants who earned a living in the packinghouses as boners, scullers, and luggers of that same livestock. Either occupation was a rugged way to make a buck.

Their unintelligible accent is but one of the many caricatures of Scots like our Bill Kinnear. They are said to be unbendingly stubborn, for example. One old trope goes like this: "You can change a

Scotsman's mind if you catch him young enough." Some find Scots gruff and discourteous. While working on a book project years ago, I came across a tidbit about the nature of Scots that still makes me smile: Early Scottish immigrants to Philadelphia supposedly infuriated the genteel Quaker population there because they refused to abide by the local tradition of "hat courtesy," whereby men were expected to doff their headwear when passing another stroller, especially women. I don't know if this is truth or myth. But I'm pretty sure I would have been one of those non-doffers, too.

Another caricature of Scots suggests that they are hardworking and industrious. This seems to have been a good description of both Kinnear and his Irish wife.

On June 2, 1900, a census-taker named Joseph Walker found the Kinnears living on S Street as homeowners "free of mortgage." That seems remarkable, since Bill Kinnear had been in the U.S. for just a decade at that point—and even more so considering the typical wages of his era. Here's the math: If small houses in their neighborhood were selling for $750 in 1899, as the newspaper ad touted, the Kinnear place likely would have been worth half again as much, say $1,100. The smaller house would have taken their investment total to at least $1,600, comparable to roughly $50,000 in 2022.

Meanwhile, laborers in South Omaha back then were earning peanuts. An article from the 1904 Quarterly Journal of Economics broke down the hourly wages by the dizzying array of graphic meatpacking specializations. Hanging beef was deconstructed on an assembly line. The most unskilled grunt laborers—luggers, lifters, and cleaners—were paid as little as 16 cents an hour, or about 10 bucks for a 60-hour week. Burly knockers, who killed beef cows with a blow to the forehead with their eight-pound sledgehammers, made 24 cents an hour. Specialists known as gullet-raisers, head-boners, scribe-sawyers, and tail-rippers got 20 cents an hour; foot-skinners and bruise-trimmers 22½; leg-breakers and breast-sawyers

The Kinnears in the 1900 Census

25 cents, and neck-splitters 31½. Even "rumpers," who earned top wages of 40 cents an hour, took home less than $25 for 60 hours of labor. (I'm not sure I want to know what a rumper's job entailed.)

Bill Kinnear never worked on a slaughterhouse butcher line as far as I can tell, but he did spend his early years in Omaha as a furnace-tender at the Paxton Building downtown and then at the old South Omaha Packing Company, at 30th and Q Streets, where he would have earned about $20 a week. Perhaps he brought a substantial financial stake from Scotland, although I doubt it. However they managed it, the feat that Nellie and her husband pulled off, free-and-clear homeownership so quickly, is a testament to the industriousness of this formidable immigrant couple.

SEVEN

Growing Up

BILL AND NELLIE KINNEAR'S kids grew up listening to the competing brogues of their parents. Nellie would have spoken with the mild accent of western Ireland, which most Americans have little trouble understanding. But the kids surely sometimes puzzled over their dad's words, spoken with the famously baffling trills, swallowed letters, and phlegmy "achs" of the Doric dialect of northeast Scotland. According to one example I found, if Bill Kinnear happened to be telling his children about the chilly fall weather back home, it might sound something like this: "It's aye caul in Aiberdeenshire in November, myne an hap up!" (It's always cold in Aberdeenshire in November, remember to wrap up.)

Of course, the Kinnear children would have been accustomed to hearing all manner of accents. The neighborhoods of immigrant-rich South Omaha were filled with a cacophony of languages. On their street alone, they had neighbors who hailed from Norway, Germany, England, Ireland, and a half-dozen U.S. states, including Vermont, Massachusetts, Illinois, Missouri, and Kansas, according to the 1910 federal census.

What was Bill Kinnear's personality like? I don't want to oversell clichés about the stern Scottish temperament, but stories passed down through one branch of his family suggest that Bill was a gruff and uncompromising disciplinarian—tough as a cheap steak. "I always heard that William was very strict with his kids," my cousin Don Szymanski told me. Don is the grandson of Robert Kinnear, Bill and Nellie's youngest child. (His grandfather and my grandmother were siblings.) Robert, born in 1902, lived a long life, outlasting many of his siblings by decades. Thankfully, he shared a number of family stories with his daughter, Marlene Kinnear Szymanski, who passed them along to her son Don, an avid genealogist who has documented his family's history.

Don shared with me a number of vignettes that shed light on our shared ancestors. For example, he helped clear up questions about the Kinnear family's faith. The Kinnear children were raised as Catholics, like Nellie. She and her kids became parishioners at St. Agnes, one of South Omaha's oldest Catholic parishes, founded in 1889 at 22nd and Q Streets. One by one as they reached age 6, the Kinnear offspring were enrolled in the grade school there. For the first generation of the McAuliffe-Kinnears in America, every significant family event happened at St. Agnes—weddings, Baptisms, graduations, and funerals.

Catholicism was rather rare in Scotland. William likely grew up attending Presbyterian services of the Church of Scotland in the Fyvie vicinity. (The nearest Catholic church was 25 miles away in Aberdeen, a day's ride by wagon or a journey of several hours via the Great North of Scotland Railway.) I wondered whether Bill Kinnear was a Catholic convert but believed that this detail was bound to be another missing brick in this history—until I spoke with Don Szymanski.

"According to what I've been told, William converted to Catholicism only on his deathbed," Don told me. "The family lore is that he was sometimes supposed to go to church—to meet his family there—but he always somehow got lost along the way, and that would get him in big trouble with his wife." Of course, there were a couple of dozen distractions between his S Street home and St.

Agnes. Could you blame a workingman for taking a wrong run into a Q Street saloon on his day off?

The church was nine blocks east of the Kinnear home — down a slope, over the low-lying railyards, then back up the other side. This trip to church by Nellie and her kids would have been a colorful and odiferous Sunday morning jaunt along Q Street — whether on foot or by streetcar — past the rugged taverns and looming meat plants. The soundtrack would have included the doleful cries of doomed live-stock penned nearby, awaiting their fate at the packinghouses. They might also have passed men heading home from an overnight shift, still wearing bloody aprons or butchers' coats, a common sight on Q Street for decades. And then there was the ever-present and unmis-takable scent of South Omaha — manure from the stockyard pens and chutes, the iron-tinted smell of blood from packinghouse ex-haust, a little engine oil, a hint of sulfur from coal furnaces.

But don't call it a stink. "It's the smell of money," South Omaha old-timers would say. "You get used to it."

Our first-generation immigrant ancestors had no choice but to get used to it. Bill and Nellie staked their family's place in America in the very midst of the packinghouse district, two blocks from the cor-ner of 30th and Q, an epicenter of the industry. Eventually, meat plants would nearly surround the neighborhood — with multi-story brick monoliths within six or fewer city blocks to the northwest, due north, northeast, due east, and southeast. And for decades to come, the Stockyards and its adjacent meatpacking plants and affiliated in-dustries would serve as financial anchors for the Kinnear kids and dozens of their descendants, from one generation to the next.

 ON A WARM LATE-SPRING DAY in 1911, the first in se-ries of losses befell the Kinnear family. At 17, William Jr., Nellie and Bill's oldest child, was just coming of age. Known as Billy, he had completed his elementary

schooling at St. Agnes and had gone to work in the lard department at Cudahy's packinghouse.

Like thousands of other Omahans, Billy enjoyed spending free time at Carter Lake, the U-shaped body of water — an old oxbow off the Missouri River — located just north of downtown Omaha. The south shore of the big lake was dominated by a vast amusement park, Courtland Beach, advertised as "The Coney Island of the West." It featured a rollercoaster and other thrill rides, carnival games, a restaurant, and a two-story lakeside pavilion where dance bands performed nearly every day and night.

Young Billy traveled seven or eight miles on streetcars from his South Omaha home to have a swim at Carter Lake on the afternoon of Tuesday, May 30, 1911. It was Memorial Day, back before the holiday was moved to the last Monday in May. It was seasonally warm for Omaha, with temperatures near 80. Courtland Beach was packed with hundreds of holiday revelers — some lounging on the beach, others dancing to the orchestra. As sunset approached, Billy and W.V. Runzel, a young man he apparently had just met that evening, decided to swim halfway across the big lake to a "bathing platform" — a dock. Family lore suggests that Billy was an excellent swimmer and may have worked as a lifeguard at some point in his young life, according to conversations that my cousin Nancy Keating Walsh recalled with her mother and our grandmother.

At the Kinnear dinner table on S Street that afternoon, father Bill must have intuited trouble, according to an account related to me by Don Szymanski. The father looked at an empty chair and place setting and asked, "Where's Billy at?" Told that the boy had gone swimming again, his father huffed, "Does he want to drown in the river or what?"

The next day, the *Omaha Bee* published a dramatic front-page account of poor Billy's fate:

LAD DROWNS AT CARTER LAKE

Sinks While Attempting to Swim Across the Pond.

BODY IS NOT YET RECOVERED

William Kannear of South Omaha Disappears Below the Surface in Sight of Hundreds of Spectators.

William Kannear, aged 19 years, of South Omaha, while swimming in Carter lake near Courtland beach, in full view of hundreds of spectators on the shore and several boating parties, drowned in about twenty feet of water. The accident occurred at 8 o'clock Tuesday night and at an early hour this morning the body had not been recovered.

Omaha Bee, May 31, 1911

The story said Billy had gone under in 20 feet of water "in full view of hundreds of spectators on the shore and several boating parties." The *Bee* story continued:

> He had reached a point opposite the bathing platform, which is . . . near the middle of the lake, when he gave a scream and disappeared from view . . . His companion came to his rescue, but Kinnear's body never came to the surface after sinking the first time . . . Onlookers on the shore thought Kinnear was trying to alarm his companions and paid little attention to the noise until he failed to reappear above the water . . . In the big pavilion close by, a lively waltz was being played by the orchestra, and the happy laughter of the merry dancers was heard above the screams of the drowning boy.

The *Omaha World-Herald* reported that Billy's body was recovered at about 11 P.M., "after three hours of hard work." The story continued, "In the darkness, the task of recovering the body was a hazardous one, and only the most capable of swimmers were allowed to participate in the search." To compound the Kinnear family's grief, a coroner's inquest into the drowning cited Courtland Beach's management for "gross negligence" because it had failed to heed Billy's cries and mount an urgent rescue. The Omaha newspaper said, "There was testimony at the hearing to show that it was practically one hour and a half before an effort was made to locate the boy's body, and that no effort was made early enough to save him."

William Kinnear Jr. was laid out at home and bid a tearful goodbye with a funeral Mass at St. Agnes. His drowning left an indelible mark on the family, including Billy's five siblings: They were mortified of swimming. Nancy Keating Walsh, who was very close to our grandmother, Billy's sister Eileen, said she often warned her to steer clear of ponds and swimming pools. "Grandma was terrified of the water," Nancy said, "and she told me many times that we kids should stay away from it, too." I was not surprised to learn that the same fear had been passed down through the family of Robert Kinnear. His grandson, Don Szymanski, told me, "Grandpa Bob never learned to swim, and he wouldn't let his daughter, my mother Marlene, take swimming lessons. The entire family was paranoid about water."

EIGHT

The Fighting Kinnears

THE KINNEARS WERE IN MOURNING AGAIN six years later. William Kinnear Sr., our hardworking immigrant paterfamilias, finally wore himself out. He died at home on July 4, 1918. A brief story in the *Omaha Bee* cited "heart trouble" as the cause of death. His death certificate, passed down through the family, provides a more complete picture. It seems that Bill died a torturously slow death related to a damaged heart valve. He had been under a doctor's care for a full five months before he died. The cause cited by his physician was "chronic valvular heart disease," a condition that today is fixed through fairly routine surgery to repair or replace the faulty valve. The doctor reported that interstitial nephritis, an inflammation of the kidneys, was a contributing factor to his death.

Bill Kinnear was just 57 years old when he died, having lived not quite half of his life in his adopted country. He was buried at St. Mary's Cemetery in South Omaha, like most of our early ancestors. His large, rectangular headstone sits just a few paces off Q Street, at the northern edge of the graveyard. The stone is marked with a Woodmen of the World insignia; it came as a fringe benefit of the company's cut-rate life insurance policies a century ago. The plot is just a few blocks from the home he built on S Street—a 10-minute walk. As his life came to an end, it must have given him comfort that he left his wife and family with a secure roof over their heads.

As best I can tell from city directories and censuses, Nellie Kinnear never worked outside the home after her marriage. But two years after her husband died, the 1920 census showed that her five children had stepped up to help, thanks to the availability of meat-packing jobs. Her oldest surviving child, Grace, was 24 years old, married, and out of the S Street house by then. But the other four — Eileen, 22, Harry, 20, Clara, 18, and Robert, 17 — were still living at home and had gone to work. My grandmother, Eileen, was employed as a retail clerk, and the others worked in the packing-houses. Harry and his kid brother, Robert, were identified in the census as laborers, and sister Clara was a "meat wrapper." (It was not unusual to find women in that line of work. Over the years, thousands of women — and many children — worked as meatpackers in Omaha, doing skilled knife work on the bacon-trimming, sausage-making, and canning lines.)

William Kinnear Dies.

William Kinnear died Thursday at the age of 58 at his residence, 3014 S street, of heart trouble. He is survived by his wife and five children, Arline, Mary, Clara, Robert Kinnear and Mrs. Grace Kleber. The funeral will be held from St. Agnes' church, Saturday at 9 a. m. Rev. James Aherne will preach the funeral sermon. Burial will be in St. Mary's cemetery.

Omaha Bee, July 5, 1918

William Kinnear's Gravestone, St. Mary's Cemetery, South Omaha

A year after that 1920 census was taken, Clara Kinnear was married. The ceremony took place in March 1921 at the courthouse in Sarpy County, south of Omaha. Clara, 21 years old on her wedding day, married Robert F. Bogatz, a young man of Czech/Polish ancestry who grew up in the Brown Park neighborhood, one of South

Omaha's Bohemian enclaves. A photo from the 1920s shows Clara, dark-haired and square-jawed, smiling beneath the brim of a big frilly hat and matching dress. Sadly, like her brother Billy, she was destined for an abbreviated life.

Clara gave birth to the first of three sons, Robert J. Bogatz, in the fall of 1921. Her second son, James, was born in 1925, and he was followed by Gerald, born on May 8, 1928. Fourteen weeks after Gerald's birth, the *True Voice*, Omaha Catholic newspaper, published this obituary:

> *Funeral services for Mrs. Clara Bogatz, aged 27, 2524 S. 25th St., who died Friday, were held on Monday morning from the residence of her mother, 3014 S Street, to St. Agnes Church at 9 o'clock. Interment was in St. Mary's Cemetery. Surviving are her husband, Robert; three sons, Robert, James and Gerald; her mother, Mrs. William Kinnear, two sisters, Grace Kleber and Mrs. Eileen Strack; two brothers, Harry and Robert Kinnear.*

Once again, a coffin holding a loved one had been set on display in the Kinnear front room. The proximity of Gerald's birth to Clara's death suggested that she had died of complications related to childbirth. A death of a mother at such a young age is unusual, and I had hoped to confirm the cause in order to give a more complete account of Clara's brief life. But I failed in my attempts to reach direct descendants who might have that information, all these years later. All three of her sons had passed on. The oldest, Robert, died in New Orleans in 1987. James died in 1989, and Gerald, who lived in Council Bluffs, was the last to go, in 2002, at age 74. I found it poignant that

Clara Kinnear Bogatz

Clara Kinnear Bogatz's gravestone at St. Mary's Cemetery, South Omaha

Gerald's obituary in the *Council Bluffs Nonpareil* named Clara Kinn-ear Bogatz, the mother he never knew. I reached out with no avail to a Bogatz niece in Wisconsin and struck out in trying to reach any of her kin in Omaha. I was about to give up when, on a hunch, I checked in with my sister-in-law, Jennifer Jaksich Krajicek. I knew that her mother's maiden name was Bogatz and that she had grown up in South Omaha. Jen put the two of us in touch, and Rejean Bo-gatz Jaksich went to work to get an answer to my question. She soon discovered that Clara's husband, Robert Bogatz, was a brother of her own grandfather, Frank Bogatz, who owned a grocery store in Brown Park. Rejean located a cousin she had never met, Nicole Bo-gatz Hanna, the daughter of Clara's middle son, James.

Ninety-four years after Clara's death, Nicole sent a message from her home in the Missouri Ozarks that recounted the details of her grandmother's untimely death. During her pregnancy, Clara had been afflicted with gestational diabetes, a potentially dangerous blood sugar spike. The condition had gone undiagnosed by Clara's doctor, Nicole said. In the weeks after Gerald was born, Clara developed a gall bladder problem — diabetics are often beset with gall stones — that required surgery to remove the organ. The combination of diabetes and the surgery took Clara's life, her granddaughter said, leaving her husband alone with three young boys. The extended Bogatz family saw to it that Clara's sons were raised properly. I trust that their mother would be happy that, a century along, her descendants remember Clara — and how she was lost to them.

Grace, second-oldest of the Kinnear kids, married Fred Kleber, a South Omaha butcher and meat market manager, in about 1918. They raised seven children and lived at 3540 South 27th Street, near C Street in South Omaha. Their children were Alice, born in 1922; Donald, 1924; Ruth, 1927; Betty, 1929; William, 1931; Richard, 1933, and Gerald, 1936. Fred died in 1947 and Grace in 1950. Their youngest son, known as Jerry, and his wife, Connie, were frequently part of the extended Kinnear family get-togethers in the 1960s and '70s.

Harry Charles Kinnear, the second-born son, had a long career as a packinghouse supervisor. But as a young man, he moonlighted in a much more interesting paying gig, as a professional prizefighter. Short but sinewy like his father, Harry was a tough kid whose passion was boxing, the sweet science. He grew up in the ring, fighting as a teenager in amateur events at South Omaha men's clubs — the Elks, the American Legion, and others. He turned professional at about age 20 and spent the first three years of the Roaring Twenties fighting as a bantamweight, roughly 118 pounds. His bouts took him as far as Ottumwa, 225 miles from home in southeastern Iowa. His ability to maintain such a light bodyweight suggests that Harry inherited his father's determination.

He was not a headliner as a fighter — lightweights rarely were — but Harry was mentioned in a dozen or so boxing stories published in the *Omaha Bee* from 1920 to 1922, often as a combatant in preliminary bouts against a regular cast of familiar foes, including "Kid" Bruno from Omaha and Yankee Sullivan from Long Pine, Nebraska. In August 1920, he fought an eight-round bout against Sullivan at the Eagles Hall at 23rd and N Streets in South Omaha. That October, he had second billing on a fight night card in Des Moines, Iowa, against a boxer from St. Paul, Minnesota. He fought in Ottumwa, Iowa, at least twice in 1921, winning a decision in April and knocking out an opponent in May. In September 1921, he had second billing in a card at the American Legion Club in Plattsmouth, Nebraska.

The pinnacle of Harry's pugilistic career came on August 12, 1921, in a five-fight match at the Omaha Municipal Auditorium, a regal building — demolished long ago — that stood at 15th and Howard Streets downtown. An advertisement touted the card as "This Season's Greatest Boxing Event." Covering the event for the *Omaha Bee*, sportswriter Ralph Wagner said the fights were held "before the largest crowd of fistic fans that has ever packed the old structure . . . Five bouts were dished out to the fans, and the show as a whole was one of the best staged in Omaha."

In covering that event, Wagner provided us with the only detailed account I found of one of Harry's bout — once again, against a well-acquainted foe:

> *Harry Kinnear won the decision over Yankee Sullivan after six rounds of boxing. This was another good scrap, furious all the way, keying up and pleasing the crowd. Sullivan fought a game battle from start to finish. Kinnear was able to connect with Sullivan, but his blows lacked the steam behind them to score a knockout.*

Don't Miss This
SEASON'S GREATEST
BOXING EVENT
Under Auspices of American Legion, Roosevelt Post No. 30

Sam Langford vs. Lee Anderson
World's Greatest Puglist — Light Heavy Weight Champion of the World (Colored)

10 Rounds

Ed "Bear Cat" Wright vs. Jack Taylor
Colored — Colored

8 Rounds

Bob Ferguson vs. Ed Hunt
4 Rounds

Jack Gates vs. Happy Malone
4 Rounds

Harry Kinnear vs. Kid Bruno
4 Rounds

OMAHA AUDITORIUM, FRIDAY EVENING, AUGUST 12
Tickets on Sale at Usual Places. Prices $1.00 to $5.00

Music by Dan Desdunes Band from 7 P. M. Until Atheletic Program Starts.

Omaha Bee, August 9, 1921 (Kinnear fought Yankee Sullivan, not Kid Bruno)

I want to point out an interesting historical footnote to this event. World War I had ended three years earlier, in 1918. More than 800 Black men from Omaha had served abroad in segregated Army units, the 92nd and 93rd Infantry Divisions. When they returned home, these men were barred from joining white American Legion clubs. So in order to rekindle the camaraderie they experienced at war, these Black men formed their own Legion club—North Omaha's Post No. 30, which they named after Theodore Roosevelt. This Legion post was the sponsor of the Municipal Auditorium fights that night, which included an integrated card of both Black and white boxers, although the races did not mix in the ring. As the newspaper advertisement shows, the two top-billed fights were Black on Black, the others white on white. Importantly, fans of any and all races were allowed to attend. Boxing was still largely segregated then, and this sort of mixing was unusual in social settings—and pretty much anywhere else in Omaha, outside of packinghouse kill floors. I imagine some white boxers might have turned down an invitation to fight under those circumstances. I admire Harry for taking part.

The last record I found of Harry's boxing career was a brief advance item published in the *Bee* on November 29, 1922. Harry was fighting that week at the Cudahy Athletic Club, obviously affiliated with the packinghouse.

Why did he hang up his gloves? In the summer of 1920, just as his professional prize-fighting career was taking off, Harry had married Nellie O'Brien, an Iowa-born young woman of Irish stock. I don't imagine that his new bride was thrilled about her husband's boxing gigs, but she endured it for most of three years. Perhaps Harry grew tired of maintaining an adolescent-sized physique.

Harry and his wife made their first home at 5212 South 38th Street, just off Q in South Omaha's Irish Hill. In the early years of his marriage, Harry was promoted to foreman at Dold Packing Company, which boasted a thoroughly modern plant when it opened in 1920 in his old Jetter's Addition neighborhood. He continued as a supervisor when Dold was sold out to Chicago-based Wilson & Company in 1938. Harry and Nellie had a single offspring, Harry Jr., born on May 2, 1925. By 1940, Harry, Nellie, and their son had left deep South Omaha for a tidy house at 4845 Pine Street, north of Center Street and adjacent to the attractive Field Club neighborhood. Harry lived a long life, dying at age 80, on Sept. 20, 1979. His wife lived into her mid-80s, dying in 1986. Harry Jr. died in 2007.

The youngest Kinnear offspring, Robert, enjoyed the longest life of all his siblings. Born on September 1, 1902, he lived for 86 years — a lifetime that spanned 16 American presidencies, from Theodore Roosevelt to George H.W. Bush. Like his siblings, Bob Kinnear finished school prematurely so he could go to work to help support his widowed mother. He must have had a close connection with Nellie. He was still living with her on S Street when the 1930 census was taken, a few months shy of his 28th birthday, and he stayed there into his early thirties, according to Omaha city directories. Those records suggest that Harry Kinnear, his ex-boxer brother, kept an eye on Bob. The two men had long parallel careers in the meatpacking industry. Bob followed Harry to a job at Dold Packing, where Bob worked as a pickle-maker in the 1930s. When Dold sold out to Wilson, the brothers (and some 800 other employees) continued their same work — Harry as a supervisor, Bob as a laborer — under a new brand of meat products.

Bob did finally get out of the S Street homeplace. On June 22, 1932, he married a young woman named Eileen Starr. The 1940 Census found them living together at 3926 R Street, among the many Hibernians of Irish Hill. They had two children, Marlene, born September 22, 1935, and William (apparently named for Bob's father and brother), born in 1939. While researching Bob Kinnear's life in old city directories, I discovered that by the late 1940s, Eileen seemed to have been replaced at the R Street house by a new wife, a telephone company employee named Catherine. A 1954 Omaha directory showed that Robert, Catherine, and his daughter Marlene, at age 19, were all still living on R Street. I also learned via family

Bob and Eileen Kinnear's Wedding Photo

lore that Bob may have spent time in a state facility in the 1960s while undergoing some sort of mental health crisis.

I wanted to know more about Bob's life, of course, so I tried to track down his daughter, Marlene. I calculated that she could very well have been alive in 2022, at age 82 or so, but my online research failed to locate her. I feared that the story of Bob, Eileen, and Catherine was going to be another missing brick in this history. But

I was soon reminded that South Omaha, despite a population of some 75,000 people, is really a tiny village where everyone are cousins. In the midst of my Kinnear research, I happened to speak with my cousin Mary Beth Keating, her family's genealogist. (Our mothers were sisters.) I mentioned my attempt to locate Marlene Kinnear, and Mary Beth surprised me by saying that she had actually met Marlene, who—as she recalled—had attended the funerals of both of her parents some years ago. She didn't recall Marlene's married surname, so I texted Mary Beth's sister Nancy Keating Walsh. Nancy texted back, "I believe it's Szymanski. I think her daughter is a friend of Linda (Keating, her sister-in-law) . . . I think they went to school together."

Sure enough. Linda put me in touch with her friend Susan Szymanski Ludlow, and a few weeks later I was on the phone with her brother Don Szymanski, son of Marlene and grandson of Bob Kinnear. Don lives in the Las Vegas area, near his mother and father, Don Sr. Although Marlene's memory is diminished, Don Jr. was able to provide valuable information and insights about the Kinnears—including a delightful story that explained how and why a woman named Catherine seemed to have replaced his wife, Eileen Starr, in Bob Kinnear's life.

There was no marital hanky-panky—Eileen and Catherine were the same person. Don explained that when Eileen Starr was an underaged teen, she applied for a job at the local phone company using the name and birthdate of her sister, Catherine, older by two years, because she knew she was too young to be hired. The name Catherine then trailed her through life, including in city directories that I found from the late 1940s through mid-1950s, decades after she told the little white lie to get a job.

I asked Don whether he had met his grandfather.

"Sure," he told me. "He lived in our basement when I was a little boy. I remember him as being a very feisty man. He wasn't very tall, and he liked to drink. I imagine he was pretty well acquainted with bartenders up and down Q Street."

Like his bantamweight brother Harry, Bob was a sporty kid, but his game was baseball. Don Szymanski told me that family lore suggests that Harry and Bob—known as the "Kinnear Boys"—were widely recognized in South Omaha for their athleticism. Don said that while Harry was known as a fine fighter, a story passed down through his family suggested he (or his manager) weren't above concealing a well-placed piece of iron to his gloves to add a little oomph to his punch. "There was one particular fight that Harry was losing where his cornerman slipped something into his glove, and Harry ended up winning," Don said. "They say the guys who knew about that trick laughed about it at the Q Street bars for years afterward."

Bob Kinnear had his own brush with sports fame. He played shortstop on a neighborhood team that included several brothers from a bookmaking family named Gaughan that lived on his block. The youngest of the Gaughan brothers, Jackie, grew up to be a gambling-industry pioneer who moved to Las Vegas in 1950, when the town was little more than a sandy desert mirage. He eventually owned stakes in half of Sin City's casinos, including the Flamingo, Golden Nugget, Showboat, and El Cortez. "It's kind of fun that way back when in South Omaha," Don Szymanski told me, "Jackie Gaughan used to be my grandpa's batboy."

The details have been lost to time, but Bob Kinnear's stay at a mental health facility in Hastings, Nebraska, 150 miles west of Omaha, in the 1960s has been recorded in family lore. Don said he was aware that his Grandpa Kinnear had been sent away but did not know what triggered his confinement. Who knows? As Don noted, he was full of spirit and spunk—and a shot or two of whiskey. My cousin Nancy Keating Walsh recalled that our grandmother, Bob's older sister Eileen, took trips to Hastings to visit her brother. "Nobody talked about why he was there, and I was too young to figure it out," Nancy told me.

Toward the end of her life in the mid-1970s, our Grandma Eileen and her brother Bob were drawn back together by what may or may not have been coincidence. Grandma, ill with cancer and in need of 24-hour care, was living at Lucas Hall, a low-income retirement home at 36th and Cummings Street in central Omaha. And who should also happen to be living there? Brother Bob. Don Szymanski told me, "My grandpa said he wanted to move there because his sister was living there."

Even then, when he was well into his 70s, it apparently didn't take much to get Bob Kinnear's Irish up. My cousin Nancy recalled from her visits to our grandmother at Lucas Hall that Bob had an ongoing battle with another resident. Nancy said Grandma Strack cautioned her to stay away from her brother. "Don't talk to him," she said. "He's crazy."

Bob Kinnear may have been crazy, but he kind of got the last laugh. As I noted, he was by far the most long-lived of the six Kinnear siblings, with a lifetime that nearly spanned the 20th Century. He survived to age 86, dying on June 13, 1989. Don Szymanski told me that his grandfather's feistiness continued well into his dotage. "Later on, when he was living at another care center, he used to get in fights all the time with some other old man who was a resident there."

As his grandson summarized it, "Grandpa Bob lived a good long life."

And you have to admire that he went down swinging.

NINE

Our Sassy Grandma

FOR MOST OF US WHO KNEW HER, Eileen Kinnear Strack's "crazy" jab at her brother is a pretty good representation of her personality. Our grandmother was a plain-spoken woman with plenty of opinions, and she never held back from letting you know what they were — probably much like her own mother and father. Eileen was not a particularly tender grandma — not one of those *my-grandbabies-are-so-special* kind of ladies. She was more of a kid-teaser than a kid-coddler. She could be stern, but she also had an exuberant sense of humor. Her hee-hee-hee laugh could make window glass shimmy, although her idea of what was funny sometimes diverged from mine. Eileen had more than 30 grandkids, and family gatherings at her house could be raucous. She would sometimes lock us all out of the house. "Go play outside," she would screech. At one such event, on a warm summer day, several of us pleaded to get back inside. I think I had to pee, and others wanted a glass of water. After ignoring us for 10 or 15 minutes as we wailed at a locked screen door, Grandma suddenly rushed to the door holding two jumbo tumblers of water. But they were not to quench our thirsts. She hurled the water at us through the screen, then stood cackling, her mouth agape and head thrown back. (Yes, in my mind it was a

Wicked Witch of the West laugh.) Grandma seemed to think that her water toss was the funniest gag ever. I disagreed at the time, although her weird antic seems marginally more humorous after 60 years of seasoning—or soaking.

Eileen Strack with daughters Helen (left) and Petty in about 1940

So before I over-disparage my Grandma, let me share what I have learned about her early life—details that might help sand down the sharp edges of her personality. Eileen Marie Kinnear was Nellie and Bill's third child, born on February 27, 1897. She toddled into the new century and, like her siblings, attended Catholic grade school at St. Agnes. She didn't bother with high school. (In 1940, she confirmed to a federal census-taker that she had an eighth-grade education.) Eileen finished at St. Agnes in about 1911, when she would have been 14, and went straight from grade school to work. This was not uncommon then. Even today, federal labor laws allow 14-year-olds to work in many types of jobs.

The brief Kinnear family history that I have cited several times reported that Eileen and her older sister, Grace, helped out at the boardinghouse operated by their mother Nellie's old Irish friend, Bridget Murphy Furlong. That likely was our grandma's first job. It's interesting that the Kinnear history specifically noted that Bridget often shared with Eileen and Grace stories of her life in Ireland while they were working at her boardinghouse. This suggests that their own Irish immigrant mother, Nellie, wasn't really interested in talking about the life she left behind.

There were more horses than automobiles on South Omaha's streets in Eileen's early childhood, but all of the Kinnear children would have been accustomed to navigating the city via the streetcar lines that once traced their way around Omaha, before they were re-placed by buses. Bridget and her big family had moved out of their tiny Jetter's Addition home and into a two-story at 4115 South 23rd Street, just up the hill from Spring Lake Park. That would have been a long walk from Eileen's home on S Street, but it was a breeze by streetcar—east six blocks on Q Street, then due north for a couple miles along busy 24th Street, South Omaha's long commercial strip.

Eileen put her streetcar chops to work after finishing her education. As a single young female in her teens, she began what would be an extended professional life as a retail clerk. She worked for more than five years at Hayden Brothers Department Store in the bustling heart of downtown Omaha, at the corner of 16th and Dodge Streets. She commuted there every workday, beginning when she was about 16 and continuing into her early 20s. It's noteworthy that Eileen took a job as a retail clerk miles from home rather than trudging to one of the packinghouses right there in her neighborhood. Carving up animal flesh on an assembly line mustn't have appealed to her. By contrast, working at Hayden Brothers must have been exciting and life-expanding, bringing Eileen into daily contact with the city's elite professional class. Hayden Brothers, founded in the late 1880s by Irish immigrants, competed with Brandeis, a block away at 16th and Douglas, as Omaha's toniest department stores. Both were giant enterprises spread out over multiple stories. Hayden Brothers bragged of 28 departments—everything from fine jewelry to coal—covering 40,000 square feet, about the size of a football field. In full adulthood, our Grandma Eileen was a bold, assertive woman who laughed easily. I have to think that her self-confidence had roots in her years mixing it up in downtown Omaha with customers and colleagues at Hayden Brothers.

The R.L. Polk City Directory for Omaha recorded Eileen working as a sales clerk or cashier at Hayden Brothers from at least 1915 until 1920. She was no temp; five or six years was a career. The store was literally halfway across the city—more than six miles from home and roughly an hour each day for the roundtrip ride. She paid a streetcar fare of a dime a day—a nickel each way—to get to a job that paid about ten bucks a week. In a sense, though, she was doing family duty. Eileen and her siblings supported their mother after Bill Kinnear Sr. died. Sometime in late 1920, Eileen shortened her commute, quitting Hayden Brothers to take a clerk's position at Rudoph Dietz, South Omaha's largest grocery store and meat market, at 24th and N Streets, just 10 blocks from home. As she switched jobs, other big changes were happening in the life of our future grandmother.

THE ORIGIN STORY OF THE ROMANCE between Eileen Kinnear and Harry Strack is another missing brick in this story. I do know that they were not schoolmates, nor did they grow up in the same neighborhood. By the time they met, probably in 1920, Harry had traveled a rather wobbly path through life. He came from an unstable family, and as a boy he often lived not with his parents but with various relatives, including his destitute grandparents in Council Bluffs, Iowa, his hometown. At the time he met Eileen, Harry was living with his mother and his older half-sister's family in an apartment in downtown Omaha. He had just finished a grudging, two-year stint in the military that was the government's idea, not his. It was an eight-block walk from Harry's place to Hayden Brothers. It's not impossible to imagine that Eileen caught his eye while he was shopping there.

Harry Albert Strack was born in Council Bluffs on July 8, 1895. His father was a man of German ancestry who was born in Pennsylvania in the late 1840s and migrated west, apparently following members of his extended family to Iowa. I had always understood that Harry's father had lived a ghostly life, leaving few tracks to indicate where he was from — and where the hell he went. According to family lore, he didn't stick around long enough to tell his own origin story, and when he left, he seemed to have disappeared. Strack abandoned his wife and son and was never heard from again, or so the family story goes. We knew so little about him that it took some digging for me to confirm his first name, which proved to be John. Even today, John Strack is very hard to find in the seemingly bottomless reservoir of genealogical information available online — including the normally comprehensive and reliable federal

censuses. But after some digging, I was able to fill in quite a few details about his life. And it turns out that John Strack was not quite as
elusive as we were led to believe. But as you will see, I discovered a
surprising twist in my great-grandfather Strack's biography that
might help explain his obscured past.

Early in my search, lacking such essential details as his birth and
death dates, I had to use DNA sleuthing to approximate his ancestral roots. In federal censuses, his son Harry consistently told census-takers that his father hailed from Pennsylvania — a good clue.
Strack is a German surname, from the German word meaning
straight, upright, stiff — or stubborn. (So our shared genetics deliver
a double shot of stubbornness, Scottish *and* German.)

The Strack name is common among the German immigrant stock
in the Pennsylvania Dutch region, across a wide swath of the south-
central and southeast portions of that state. Many Stracks still live
there today, descendants from the Germans and Swiss who began
leaving Europe before the American Revolution, seeking freedom
to practice their protestant faiths, including the Amish, Lutherans,
Mennonites, and Moravians. Likewise, Strack remains a familiar
surname today in Germany and its border regions with France and
Switzerland. Since having my DNA analyzed about a decade ago,
I've puzzled over my strong ancestral links to parts of Germany, as
well as to nearby Bern, Switzerland. I assumed this came from my
Strack blood but had no real evidence. This changed when I learned
that my cousin Nick Keating had had his DNA analyzed. Nick and
I were born seven weeks apart (he's older), and we share a partial
DNA profile through our mothers, sisters Helen and Eileen (Petty)
Strack. From his father and maternal grandmother, Nick's ancestry
is pure Scottish and Irish. But when I overlayed the map of his geo-
graphical ancestral DNA with mine, Nick and I shared identical
roots in the same areas of Germany and Switzerland, suggesting

that our maternal great-grandfather was descended from Germanic immigrants from that region.

IN THE EARLY 1890s, while living in the Omaha-Council Bluffs area, John Strack met and a married a woman named Mary Elizabeth Gibler Beasley, a divorcee with a young daughter. I'm reminded of my sister Colleen Krajicek's question about our unknown ancestors: "Why didn't we know these people?" Mary was our maternal great-grandmother, and she lived out her life across the river from us in Council Bluffs, where she is buried at Walnut Hill Cemetery. But I trust that not a single living descendant from the Strack line would even recognize her name. So let me fill in some details of her rather interesting life.

Mary was born on October 4, 1857. Her tombstone in Council Bluffs says she was born in 1860, but that is wrong. Records show that she was nearly 3 years old at the time of the federal census of 1860. She came from Midwestern stock. Her father, John Newtown Gibler, was a farmer who was born on May 22, 1831, in Fincastle, Ohio, a hamlet 50 miles east of Cincinnati. In the early 1850s, Gibler moved 500 miles west, to Jones County, Iowa, northeast of Cedar Rapids. Iowa had been granted statehood in 1846, so he likely was attracted by the prospect of cheap farmland and a stable government. On September 20, 1854, Gibler married Martha Jane Farris, a teenager born in about 1836 in Boonville, Indiana. Hers was a true Iowa pioneer family, having moved there even before statehood. John and Martha Gibler got to work helping to populate America's 29th state. Records show that Martha gave birth to as many as 15 children, although at least two died in infancy. At the time of the 1860 federal census, as the Civil War began, John Gibler and his growing family were living in northeastern Iowa and seemed to be on the road to prosperity. He was listed as a land-owning farmer, with a modest-sized property valued at $300, equivalent to more than $10,000 today.

If the origins of our great-grandfather John Strack are a mystery, the family history of the woman he married is quite a different story. I discovered that we had Gibler ancestors who were living five centuries ago in the Rhineland region of what is now western Germany. This takes that branch of our family back to the beginning of the Renaissance, to about the time that DaVinci painted the Mona Lisa and Michelangelo was at work on the ceiling of the Sistine Chapel in Rome.

John Gibler's father was James David Gibler, born in 1804 in Brown, Ohio, and died in 1886 in Mercer, Missouri. His grandfather, another John Gibler, was born in 1781 in the Shenandoah Valley of Virginia and died in 1829 in Ohio. He was another testament to that family's fertility: Records show he had as many as 14 siblings, then fathered 13 children with his wife, Rosanna Layman Gibler.

The Gibler family lived for several generations in the vicinity of Shenadoah, Virginia, 20 miles east of Harrisonburg, on what was then one of America's western frontiers. Yet another John Gibler lived out his life there, born in 1759 and died in 1826. His father, Christian Gibler, was born in 1720 in the German Rhineland (then the Kingdom of Prussia). He married Anna Latsch in 1748, and the couple emigrated to America a few years later and made their way to Shenandoah. Like their heirs, Christian and Anna had a Gibler-sized family — about 12 children. Both Christian (1787) and Anna (1780) died in Shenandoah, Virginia.

After emigrating, Christian had shortened his Germanic surname from Giebeler to Gibler. Going back even further in the old country, the family's male line included Christian's father, Johannes Giebeler, 1694 to 1722; George Giebeler, 1641 to 1720; Hayn

Harry Strack's Family Tree

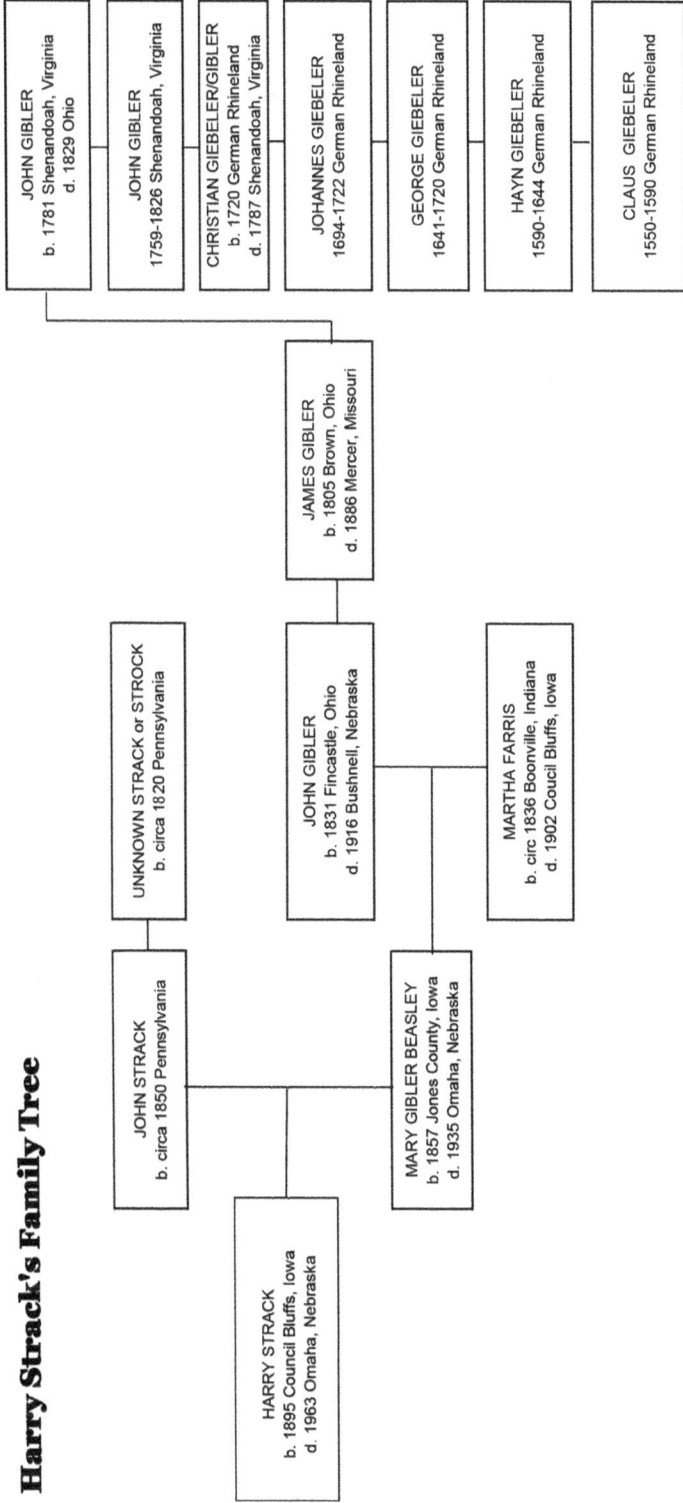

JOHN GIBLER
b. 1781 Shenandoah, Virginia
d. 1829 Ohio

JOHN GIBLER
1759-1826 Shenandoah, Virginia

CHRISTIAN GIEBELER/GIBLER
b. 1720 German Rhineland
d. 1787 Shenandoah, Virginia

JOHANNES GIEBELER
1694-1722 German Rhineland

GEORGE GIEBELER
1641-1720 German Rhineland

HAYN GIEBELER
1590-1644 German Rhineland

CLAUS GIEBELER
1550-1590 German Rhineland

JAMES GIBLER
b. 1805 Brown, Ohio
d. 1886 Mercer, Missouri

UNKNOWN STRACK or STROCK
b. circa 1820 Pennsylvania

JOHN GIBLER
b. 1831 Fincastle, Ohio
d. 1916 Bushnell, Nebraska

MARTHA FARRIS
b. circ 1836 Boonville, Indiana
d. 1902 Coucil Bluffs, Iowa

JOHN STRACK
b. circa 1850 Pennsylvania

MARY GIBLER BEASLEY
b. 1857 Jones County, Iowa
d. 1935 Omaha, Nebraska

HARRY STRACK
b. 1895 Council Bluffs, Iowa
d. 1963 Omaha, Nebraska

Giebeler, 1590 to 1644, and Claus Giebeler, 1550 to 1590. Thus, our distant ancestor Claus was born 31 years after DaVinci died, and his life overlapped with Michelangelo. He would have 14 years old when the great Italian sculpture and painter died in 1564.

TEN

'Unknown Beasley' Revealed

RACING FORWARD 300 YEARS from Michelangelo's Rome to rural Iowa, prosperity seems to have been fleeting at John Gibler's farm. The 1880 census found that the Giblers had abandoned Jones County, Iowa, and moved their huge brood to Shenandoah, a farm town in southwestern Iowa, 60 miles from Omaha-Council Bluffs. The census reported that John was a farm laborer, not the land-owning farmer he was 20 years earlier. By 1882, the family had relo-cated again—to a neighborhood of tiny shacks within spitting dis-tance of the big, gritty Council Bluffs railyard, where John had gone to work. From the door of their home, the Giblers could have seen the fancy depot and hotel that had become the thrumming hub of the Bluffs. But it was a world apart. Quite literally, the Giblers lived on wrong side of the tracks.

Our ancestor Mary Gibler, second-oldest of the 15 children, was unmarried and in her mid-20s when her family arrived in Council Bluffs. But within months of arriving in the booming railroad town, she had found a man—or a man had found her. On Christmas Day 1882, our Harry Strack's future mother got married in Council Bluffs to her first husband—a mysterious fellow named Beasley.

EVERYONE HAS A STORY to tell. That has been my mantra over a long career as a writer, dating to my first paid reporting job at the *Council Bluffs Nonpareil* in the late 1970s. A few years ago, I followed that self-advice and published a nonfiction book called *Dear Mama,* in which I reconstructed the life story of my paternal grandmother, Hazel Chandler Krajicek, who abandoned my father when he was a boy. I am proud of my research on that book, and I have tried to apply that lesson here—to go deeper in my inquiries than might seem reasonable to try to tell as fully as possible the life stories of these people, strangers to virtually everyone reading this. There are many dozens of people named herein, and no doubt many of them, like our immigrant ancestors Nellie McAuliffe and Bill Kinnear, traveled interesting paths through life. But some stand out, and one of them was this man named Beasley, the first husband of our Harry Strack's twice-married mother. Beasley is not directly related to us, but his life story is worth a little sidetrack trip. The man was a doozy.

Through several rounds of records research, I had learned almost nothing about Beasley—not even his first name. He was so obscure in online records that he was listed as Mary's husband by the name "Unknown Beasley." Yet I was fixated on identifying him, even though he's just a footnote in this book. Perhaps I was spurred on by the gaze of my Grandma Hazel Krajicek's ghost, peering over my shoulder. Whatever the inspiration, I decided to give it one more time-wasting try as I was finishing up a first draft of this manuscript. I tried a new search on myheritage.com—a valuable resource—for the Beasley surname paired with common first names—William, Robert, etc. My third attempt was with the forename John—and bingo. His name was John Beasley, and I soon learned that he was a native of Illinois, having grown up in the small town of Union, midway between Chicago and Rockford. I also learned that there was a significant age difference between Beasley and Mary Gibler when they were married in the Bluffs on Christmas Day in 1882: At 40, Beasley was a full 15 years older than his bride. Two years after they were wed, Mary got pregnant. On June 17, 1885, she gave birth to a daughter that she named Cora May (or Cora Mae, in some records). So I now had these basic facts about John and Mary's relationship, and I knew that she was single again by 1889, when she married a second time, to John Strack. But what happened to Beasley? Did he die? Leave her for another woman? Go to prison?

I searched Omaha and Council Bluffs newspaper archives from 1880 to 1900 to see whether Beasley's appeared in an obituary. And that is where I learned that old Unknown Beasley certainly did have a story worth telling. Within two years of the birth of Cora May, Mary Gibler Beasley had legally jettisoned the baby's father from her life. A brief story in the *Council Bluffs Nonpareil* on May 7, 1887, reported that Mary's petition for divorce had been granted. The item said that her "absent consort, John, can claim her no more as his wife." It explained that John Beasley had lived in Council Bluffs "only a short time. He has now been absent from his wife and child a year and a half."

It turned out that John Beasley was an experienced hand at both marriage and hit-and-run paternity by the time he met Mary in Council Bluffs. I discovered that Beasley first said "I do" as a young man in his Illinois hometown. He married Susan Doty in 1861, when he was 20 years old. She bore him two daughters, Nellie and Florence, before he took a powder. By the time those two girls were old enough for school, Beasley had moved on to his second wife and family. In 1868 in Illinois, he married Rebecca Houghland Lidikay, a widowed mother of four. That marriage, which produced three more children, John Jr., (another) Nellie, and Felix, was finished within a decade.

Beasley then moved west, hooked up with Mary Gibler in Council Bluffs, fathered Cora May — and was gone again while the child was "a tiny infant." I know that because John Beasley's final exit made the newspapers. It turns out that after he had abandoned Mary and their daughter, Beasley had gone south to Carbondale, Kansas, where he was living in 1893. Cora May was seven years old by then, and he had not seen his child since a few months after her birth. That winter, Beasley decided to take a 250-mile train trip to Council Bluffs from his home south of Topeka. A story in the *Omaha World-Herald*, published on January 22, 1893, described what transpired on the trip. It also revealed that the thrice-married Illinois native had a title that I was not expecting:

> *Dr. John Beasley of Carbondale, Kansas, died here [in Council Bluffs] very suddenly at 2 o'clock yesterday from the effects of what was pronounced by the attending physician as enlargement of the liver. He was 53 years old. Dr. Beasley came here two days ago to visit his 7-year-old daughter, whom he had not seen for a number of years. She was staying with her grandparents, Mr. and Mrs. [John] Gibler, at the corner of Fourteenth Avenue and Thirteenth Street. He was taken sick on the train and died soon after reaching here.*
>
> *Dr. Beasley was a man in good circumstances and appears to have little knowledge of the situation of the daughter, the grandparents being very poor and their home being a small cottage destitute of most of the comforts of life. The deceased was a member of the Masonic fraternity.*

A Mason — how very upstanding. A *Nonpareil* story added that Dr. Beasley "intended visiting here awhile and then go on east to see some friends." I wonder whether he was planning to see his other former families along the way. It's fascinating to me, as a longtime newspaperman, that these news stories essentially offered an excuse for a physician who clearly had deserted his daughter. He was wealthy — "in good circumstances" — and his daughter was living in impoverished squalor. But the papers gave him cover by saying he had "little knowledge of the situation." What a load of crap. I think Beasley was a deadbeat drunk. He was living in Kansas with John Jr., his teenage son from his second marriage, who would go on to become a doctor himself. Was Beasley Sr. a legit doctor or a pretender? Formal licensing and oversight of doctors was firmly established in the United States by the early 1800s. By 1893, more than three decades after Kansas gained statehood, Beasley Sr. surely would have had to have been licensed by the state. I found an old newspaper clip that called him "the top physician" in Carbondale, Kansas.

That may have been so, but he was a lousy father with a fatal dependence on alcohol. "Enlargement of the liver," the cause of death cited in the news stories, is often the result of alcohol abuse. A follow-up story in the *Nonpareil* said an autopsy showed Beasley was afflicted with advanced peritonitis, an internal inflammation often associated with cirrhosis of the liver — a classic result of chronic boozing. Mary Gibler, a poor farm girl from a family of uneducated laborers, must have thought she'd found quite a catch in Doc Beasley. But she learned the hard way that money and morality don't necessarily go hand-in-hand. Imagine the psychological scars Beasley brought to the life of little Cora May. She was witness to the death of her father during his very first visit since her infancy.

Likewise, I feel sympathy for John and Martha Gibler, Cora's grandparents. Poor Martha, after delivering 15 babies, was then tasked with raising her granddaughter — only to be called out publicly in the newspapers for her destitution, as though she bore some responsibility for Dr. Deadbeat's death. In all likelihood, she had been pressed into the service of caring for Cora May because by 1893, daughter Mary was on the arm of her next husband, another seemingly wayward fellow named John Strack. But was she any better off?

ELEVEN

Blue Denim City

ALTHOUGH IT IS OVERSHADOWED by its much larger Nebraska neighbor across the river, Council Bluffs has long had its own distinct identity as a railroad town. The nickname is forgotten now, but a century ago it was known as Blue Denim City, after the work clothes of railroaders. President Lincoln cast in steel the Bluffs' position as an American rail fulcrum by designating the city as the eastern terminus of the transcontinental railroad, the momentous effort to link the east and west coasts of the United States. The terminus designation meant that the Bluffs functioned as the narrow spout connecting a two-sided funnel. The Union Pacific Railroad was dominant in the western half of the country, and seven different mainline railroads served the eastern United States. As the official terminus between east and west, Council Bluffs was the transfer point for human and inert cargo between Union Pacific cars and those of the eastern railroads. And the hub of this bustling terminus was the Union Pacific Transfer Depot and Hotel, a handsome brick building at Twelfth Avenue and 21st Street that overlooked the steel-laced sprawl of the railyards. This venue was known for generations as simply the Transfer, and it was the epicenter of Blue Denim City.

The depot began welcoming travelers in 1878, four years before the Giblers arrived in the Bluffs. "The West Begins Here," a big sign in the waiting room declared. The Union Pacific crowed that the Transfer had "the finest and largest bar between Chicago and Denver." In addition to repair facilities and countless sidetracks, the railyard featured a separate building that housed a massive mail-sorting operation. Council Bluffs was the funnel through which virtually all of America's cross-country mail had to pass. Government protocols required that bags of letters and parcels had to be unloaded from western railcars and transferred to eastern railcars — and vice versa.

The opening of the railroad terminal prompted a boom in Council Bluffs that rivaled that of South Omaha's meatpacking district. The population of the Iowa city increased tenfold between 1860 and 1890, from 2,000 to more than 20,000. The railroads brought prosperity to the growing town — or at least to

The Union Pacific Transfer, Council Bluffs, Iowa

parts of it. A few dozen handsome mansions went up downtown, a mile from the railyards. Many still stand today, designated as being worthy of eternal preservation. Our people didn't live in those places. They lived tight to the railyards in a neighborhood of rutted dirt streets that smelled of coal, grease, and overfilled latrines. You won't find many of these neighborhoods intact today. Most were bulldozed decades ago and replaced by industrial buildings.

I worked as a reporter for the *Council Bluffs Nonpareil* early in my career, covering cops and courts. The young reporting staff there was made up mostly of smart-ass imports (like me) from Omaha or larger cities in Iowa—Des Moines, Ames, Iowa City. I admit that we looked down our noses at the Bluffs. It was different in some intangible sense—shifty and scheming. I grew up in South Omaha, which offered every form of crime and vice known to humanity if you knew where to look. But the Bluffs seemed next-level unscrupulous to me, a carny kind of town. Every dog you saw on Broadway was missing a leg, every man limped, and every woman was wearing a crooked dime-store wig, too much perfume, and a come-hither smile. Or so it seemed.

But was it always so criminal and cockeyed? Trying to check my biases, I looked back at news clippings from around 1900 and founds lots of stories about lawlessness in the Bluffs railyard neighborhoods—women in states of "bestial intoxication" and "slinks and sneaks" angling to make a buck from one fraud or another. In the winter of 1893, a story from Council Bluffs reported that cold weather was driving an epidemic of coal-stealing. The following year, poultry theft was the crime du jour as local police reported a confiscation of metal hooks specifically designed to yank chickens out of coops. I've spent my life writing about crime, from the grandest to the most petty, and that was the first I had heard of the criminal art of wielding chicken-grabbing hooks.

David J. Krajicek

On January 3, 1895, the *Omaha World-Herald* carried this headline on its Council Bluffs news wrap-up:

THIEVING OF ALL KINDS BECOMES MORE FREQUENT AS PEOPLE FEEL THE PINCH OF POVERTY

Scores of People Who Will Steal Rather Than See Their Families Suffer the Pangs of Hunger

The story reported a flurry of arrests, including those of a man nabbed for swiping two cans of oysters from a grocery store near the railyard and a boy for swiping a lead pipe from the ruins of an old hotel. "It is evident that this class of crime is to become frequent," the story said. "People are hungry, ill-clothed and desperate, and they will steal rather than starve."

In 1903, this *Nonpareil* headline about railyard crime got right to the point:

BURGLARS! THIEVES! ROBBERS!

IN 1895, the year our Grandfather Harry Strack was born there, as many as 40 trains arrived and departed through the Council Bluffs rail funnel every day, bringing thousands of people—and fresh trouble—to Blue Denim City. I don't know precisely when Harry's father, John Strack, joined that throng, but I know he was living in the vicinity by the late 1880s, when he was about 40 years old. Historic records maintained by the State of Nebraska show that Mary Gibler Beasley married Strack on Saturday, December 28, 1889—her second Christmastime wedding. They were wed in Omaha by G. W. Shields, a Douglas County Court

```
WIRICK, Cassius M.           Dec.28,1889
   Cora Kynearson            Rob't Wheeler, Minister

STRACK, John M.              Dec.28,1889
   Mary Gibbler              G. W. Shields, Co. Judge

FLEMING, Albert              Dec.30,1889
   Priscilla Mutum           Charles Brandes, J.P.

FISHER, Thomas A.            Dec.30,1889
   Sarah C. Dunham           N. M. Mann, Minister

JEWETT, Geo. L.              Jan.1,1890
   Lucy A. High              A. Mart, J.P.
```

John Strack and Mary Gibler's marriage record—with her name misspelled

judge. That was 2½ years after she had divorced Beasley. The couple had just one child — our Grandpa Harry Strack. His mother was pushing 40 when our Harry arrived in the world.

Again, the family lore holds that John Strack was a come-and-go man — that he came to town, had a fling with Mary, fathered Harry, and was soon gone, like Mary's first husband, sleazy Doc Beasley. But the five-year lag between the marriage and Harry's birth proves that they were partners — or at least in proximity to one another — for much longer than the lore suggests. In fact, I found evidence that John Strack was solidly grounded in Council Bluffs. He appears to have lived there for at least 14 years, from his marriage in 1889 until 1903. Over a span of six or seven years around the turn of the 20th century, his name appeared in the *Nonpareil* nearly a dozen times. I was surprised to find that he was involved in local politics. For several years in the mid-1890s, he was elected as a delegate to the county Democratic convention from Ward 5 in the Bluffs, which would have meant that he was a registered voter — another sign of his grounding there. From 1898 to 1900, he served as Council Bluffs city poundmaster, in charge of wrangling stray dogs and livestock in what would have been a paid political patronage job. (He may not have been very good at it: in 1899, he was reappointed to a new term on a narrow

5-to-3 vote by the local city council.) In the first few years of the 1900s, Strack was very active in the Knights of the Maccabees, a national fraternal organization that was known for offering low-cost life insurance to its members. The *Nonpareil* reported Strack's election to several official positions with Council Bluffs Tent No. 32 of the Maccebees, including lieutenant commander and master-at-arms.

I also found a John Strack listed for more than a decade in the R.L. Polk City Directory for Council Bluffs, which documents the names, occupations, and home addresses of residents. In 1888, the Polk directory for Omaha listed a blacksmith named John Strack as a boarder at the B & M Hotel in that city. I don't know for certain if that was our John Strack, but it seems likely since our ancestor married Mary Gibler Beasley in Omaha the following year.

Three years later, in the 1891-92 edition, John Strack showed up for the first time in the Council Bluffs directory. He was living at 1512 Tenth Avenue in the Bluffs and working as a laborer at the Union Pacific railyards. Strack was at that same address through 1895, the year of his son Harry's birth, and he had continued to work as a railroad grunt. After Harry was born, Strack moved to another house a block away, 1528 Eleventh Avenue, where he was listed in the 1895-96 and 1897-98 directories. He had elevated his job status from general laborer to "wiper," a grease-and-grime position in

> Fifth Ward, First Precinct--John Brogue, C. J. Dobbins, C. A. Machan, William Lenahan, John Costelo, William Morris, C. Fitzpatrick, J. W. Bell.
> Fifth Ward, Second Precinct--Andrew Howard, John O'Brien, Chris Faul, John Strack, Wm. Grogan, John Duff.

Council Bluffs Nonpareil, 1895

> but rather brief work was made of the election, all of the old officials being re-elected. Without a dissenting vote N. C. Phillips was made city clerk; John Bates, fire chief; A. E. Avery, street commissioner; John Allwood, poll tax collector; Dr. Lacey, city physician, and Barton Nelson, custodian of the city building. John M. Strack was placed in nomination as poundmaster, the present incumbent, by a vote of five the present incumbent by a vote of five to three. J. R. Dietrich was appointed deputy city clerk and F. A. Bixby chief of police.

Council Bluffs Nonpareil, 1899

which he was responsible for cleaning engine spaces and other machinery on rail cars.

In that same timeframe, I was surprised to find John Strack's name in a few more newspaper stories about a legal dispute. Apparently, he had ambitions as a real estate developer. This is from the *Nonpareil* in 1897:

> *Julius Cherniss has brought suit in the district court against Mr. and Mrs. John Strack to oust them from premises owned by him near the Transfer. He leased the premises to the defendants and took [promissory] notes in payment. They paid several of the notes and finally failed to pay, but when Cherniss attempted to oust them he . . . was beaten.*

A few months later, the *Omaha Daily Bee* gave a more detailed account of the origins of the landlord-tenant fisticuffs, which concerned an entire block of lots that Strack had agreed to buy from Cherniss:

> *A dispute that has existed for a long time between Julius Cherniss and John M. Strack found its way into the district court again yesterday. Some time ago, Cherniss sold to Strack a block of lots in Fleming Addition on the payment plan. Strack fell into arrears with the payments and Cherniss endeavored to oust him under the terms of the property contract. A side dispute arose over the location of a building which was partially on the property of Cherniss, and a threat to remove it, led to the issuance of a temporary injunction by Judge Smith, restraining him from interfering. The suit yesterday was brought by Cherniss to compel Strack to pay rent for the time he occupied the premises after he was notified to get out. The amount asked is $110.*

Despite this relatively high profile in Council Bluffs, John Strack managed to avoid federal scrutiny. Perhaps that was by design. He does not appear in the 1900 census, while he was working as poundmaster in Council Bluffs. I believe that he was born in Pennsylvania in the late 1840s, but I failed to find our great-grandfather's name in any census, from 1850 forward—although, as I noted earlier, the 1890 census was destroyed after a fire in Washington. Taken just months after Mary and John were married, that census might have offered important clues about the family roots of our mysterious ancestor—a correct age, his precise birthplace, the birthplaces of his parents, and so forth. But all those details went up in smoke.

Strangely, while I was not able to locate John or Mary Strack in the 1900 census, I did find their son, our Grandpa Harry. He was not living with his parents; he had been farmed out to his maternal grandparents, poor John and Martha Gibler, just like Harry's older half-sister, Cora May, had been as a child. In 1900, the Giblers were still residing near the Council Bluffs railyards, in a small house at 1410 Avenue U that was rented to their youngest daughter, Stella, and her husband, George Head. The census makes clear the dire financial circumstances under which our grandfather spent this part of his boyhood. George Head, identified as a 17-year-old day laborer, was listed as the head of household. His wife Stella was 18, and the young couple had an infant son, George Jr. John Gibler, 69 years old, was identified as a retired farmer who could read but not write. Neither Stella nor Martha was employed, and George Head reported that he had been employed for just six of the previous 12 months. In other words, these four adults and two children were living on the meager wages of a teenager who was out of work half the time.

But the saddest bit of information on that census sheet for the impoverished Head/Gibler/Strack household was the attempt to pinpoint Harry's age. The federal census enumerator, P.J. Ewing, visited the household on Friday, June 1, 1900. Following a script, Ewing asked a series of questions about the origins, ages, occupations, and education for each member of the household. He noted that little Harry was "at school." The child was said to be 5 years old, and his birth month was given as August 1894. In fact, he was 4, having been born on July 8, 1895. It seems that no one in Harry's household—not his grandparents, nor his Aunt Stella—knew the poor boy's correct birthday. To boot, the adults gave the census enumerator the wrong spelling of Harry's surname, which he recorded as what looks like Stukes, not Strack.

I suspect there was a change in the relationship of Harry's parents sometime shortly before the turn of the century, a year or so before the 1900 census was taken. The 1899-1900 Bluffs city directory showed that John Strack had moved to 2039 Broadway, a mile from the railyard, in what probably was a cheap hotel or rooming house along the city's main street. In 1903, his name appeared in

Young Harry Strack in the 1900 Census, listed on the last line. His age is wrong—and so is the spelling of his name.

the *Nonpareil* in a clerical accounting of district court finances in Council Bluffs. He was included in a list of citizens who had been paid $1.35 for serving on a grand jury. (We can infer from his eligibility as a grand juror that Strack was not a convicted felon—a small "yay.") In that same year, 1903, a directory showed him living downtown at 405 Willow Avenue, again probably as a boarder.

It seems that he cut out soon after that, when his name stopped appearing in city directories and the local press. In 1910, the name John Strack showed up in a public notice in the *Tribune* newspaper in McCook, another railroad town in southwestern Nebraska, halfway to Denver. Strack's name appeared in a news item reporting those with unclaimed letters sent to general delivery at the McCook post office. I don't know if that was our John Strack, but it could have been.

In addition to his ability to avoid the federal census, Strack may have obscured or confused his identity by using various middle initials in city directories and other records—John M., John N.,

GRAND JURY WITNESSES, COUNCIL BLUFFS.

Coyle, James, witness	1.35
Callaghan, James, witness	1.35
Callaghan, T. F., witness	1.35
Empson, Matsen, witness	1.35
Fagley, E. S., witness	1.35
Filter, R. A., witness	1.35
Henney, R. A., witness	1.35
Moss, Hardin, witness	3.05
Strack, John M., witness	1.35
Slack, Arthur W., witness	1.35
Wagoner, Peter, witness	1.35
Wagoner, Emily, witness	1.35
Weir, D. L., witness	1.35

Council Bluffs Nonpareil, 1903

John H., John W. That might have been the result of mistaken transcriptions of poor handwriting since the shapes of those four initials are roughly similar. But it might also have been intentional. And there was one more Strack oddity from the time just after he disappeared: The 1907 and 1908 Bluffs directory listed a John C. Strack who lived at 1006 Avenue F and worked as a fireman for the Chicago and Northwestern Railroad, a different occupation from the many that our John Strack apparently had tried. Who was John C. and how might he be related? Another missing brick.

As you may have gathered by this point, my decades of work as a writer have molded me into a dog with a bone when it comes to research: I'll keep chewing 'til I get to the marrow. But I was finally prepared to close the notebook on my investigation of John Strack. I had unearthed lots of new details about where he lived and what he did from 1888 to 1903, and I was ready to walk away, even though I was unable to resolve much about his early and late history. And then one afternoon in July 2022, I logged into 23andMe.com again to confirm the number of my DNA relatives on the website—a detail I planned to use in the concluding section of this book. The website said my tally of DNA kin was up to 1,504 as of that day, and I used the site's data software to line up those names from closest relatives to most distant based on our shared DNA segments. I scrolled down the list and was stopped cold by the 13th name. 23andMe identified the man as a third cousin. The website showed that he and I share just under 1 percent of our total DNA profile but have six matching chromosomal segments, a high number for a moderately distant relative. 23andMe said this man and I have the same great-great grandfather. And the man's name? Thomas Strock—not Strack, but Strock with a O.

What are the odds? I reached out to Strock and his wife, Loydaine, ranchers who live west of Douglas, Wyoming. I explained my research to Loydaine, who took the time to review her husband's family history. A few hours later, she sent this reply:

I think that your family may have changed their spelling of your last name! I have traced Tom's Strock family back to William Strock in Pennsylvania. His father was Daniel Strock from Chambersburg. . . . After rereading everything, I would guess you and Tom share Daniel Strock as 2nd great grandparents.

Strock vs. Strack. Both are common German surnames, the first meaning stick and the second straight or stubborn. The German pronunciation of each name is similar, and I can see how the spellings might have morphed over time. Thanks to Loydaine Strock's lead, I was able to find a wealth of information about Daniel Strock, our suspected shared ancestor. He was born March 25, 1821, among the German-rooted "Dutch" of Chambersburg, Pennsylvania, where his family had resided for several generations, dating to the mid-1700s

My new research showed that there had been confusion about the surname dating back to the family's earliest times in America. Daniel's grandfather, born in Germany in 1735, is listed in some historical records as John Henrich Strack, not Strock. I found a family tree of Daniel's father, who used the name Henry Strock, that showed 11 of his children's surnames as Strock and two as Strack. Some family trees on MyHeritage.com list the surname as both—"Strock or Strack." I also doubled back over Council Bluffs city directories that had listed our John Strack over the course of 15 years, and I now saw that his last name was rendered as John H. Streck in 1893 and John H. Strock in 1894. Typos or an intentional smudge of his identity? Who knows.

So did this revelation help me resolve the mystery of Harry's father? Not exactly. Many families of Pennsylvania-born Strocks and Stracks migrated west in the mid- to late 1800s, as the Midwest opened to settlement, and nearly all of them seemed to have several members named John. Our Daniel Strock, a farmer who changed careers and became a successful machinist, had two wives over the course of his long lifetime, and one of his sons was named John—Strock, not Strack. Late in life, Daniel followed relatives to the vicinity of Sterling, Illinois, 65 miles east of the Quad Cities. He died in Illinois in 1903.

Another line of the eastern Strock/Strack surname turns up in the 1880 census, which showed Pennsylvania natives Henry Strack, 60, and his married son John, 33, living on adjacent farms east of Muncie, Indiana. And yet another man, John Henry Strock, born in Pennsylvania in 1857, had migrated to the Sioux City, Iowa, area by the mid-1880s. He was married, died, and buried there, but he does not seem to be a close relative of ours. Other Pennsylvania-born Stracks and Strocks show up in historical records in Ohio.

The most tantalizing close connection to our John Strack comes from Tom and Loydaine Strock themselves. Loydaine told me that Tom's great-grandfather, William Strock, fought in the Civil War, then moved with his wife and four kids to a farm in Ida County, Iowa, east of Sioux City and just 100 miles north of Council Bluffs. They had a son named John Strock, but he was born in about 1875, according to federal records, making him too young to be our John Strack. Subsequent generations of that line of the Strocks kept moving farther west—to Britton, South Dakota, in the northeast corner of that state, and then on to east-central Wyoming, 1,700 miles from the family's American roots in Pennsylvania. In the late 1800s, another William Strock was living with his wife and two children—one of them named John, of course—in Warren County, Iowa, south of Des Moines. Again, that John Strock's age does not align with our Council Bluffs relative.

A couple of months after our first exchange, I spoke with Tom and Loydaine Strock by phone from their ranch in Wyoming to update them on my dead-ended research. They had a few good theories about the mysterious John Strack. Loydaine said, "Back then, before Social Security and all the other government records we have today, who was going to know if you changed your name from Strock to Strack? Or maybe someone's bad handwriting made the *O* become an *A* along the way." She added, "Or how about this: Over time, how many families have had an argument over one thing or another where the 'black sheep' goes off on his own and starts over, in a place where he's a stranger. It's been known to happen." Her husband, Tom, added, "My own grandpa, Leonard Strock, arrived alone on a horse in Douglas, Wyoming. For many decades, none of us knew he had any relatives at all. It turns he did. He just left them behind, in South Dakota." I told him it sounds like his Leonard Strock and my John Strack were kindred spirits, if not blood relatives.

So what did I gain from this one last trip down the John Strack rabbit hole, which I have visited so many times that I ought to be paying rent there? Most importantly, I met a very gracious third cousin and his wife. While I did not fully disentangle the knot of mystery in which John Strack/Strock is tightly wrapped, I was able to confirm that our Strack line is rooted in Pennsylvania Dutch country and, before that, Germany.

OUR GREAT-GREAT GRANDMOTHER Martha Gibler, Mary Beasley Strack's impoverished mother, died on September 21, 1902. She was in her mid-60s. A brief notice in the *Omaha Daily Bee* said she had died at home, at 1406 Eighth Avenue, another little shack on the wrong side of the tracks in Council Bluffs. She was buried at Walnut

Hill Cemetery in the Bluffs following a Baptist funeral service at her house. Among the list of her many surviving children was "Mrs. Mary Strack," so she apparently considered herself a married woman at that date. Martha's husband, John Gibler, outlived his younger wife by more than a decade. He died at age 85 on November 15, 1916, in Bushnell, Nebraska, a rural crossroads at the far western edge of the state, 10 miles from Wyoming. He was living there with his daughter Stella and her husband George Head, the couple with whom Harry was living in 1900 that didn't know his birthday. (Head was trying his hand at farming, although he eventually moved back to Council Bluffs.) Gibler's body was returned to the Bluffs and buried beside Martha. Poverty persisted for the couple until the very end: Their graves apparently are not marked with headstones, according to descendants who have searched Walnut Hill for their remains.

In the 1910 census and again in a city directory of that vintage, Mary Beasley Strack was listed as a widow. Yet I can find no mention of John Strack's death in public records. Obituaries for any death were quite common in local newspapers then. Martha and John Gibler, both humble people of little means, each rated local obits when they died, as did both Nellie and Bill Kinnear. Wouldn't that also be true of a man who had served as city animal catcher, who was active in local politics, and who held officer's positions in a well-known fraternal organization? But as far as I've been able to determine, our John Strack's passing drew no public notice. So did he leave his wife and flee the region, perhaps because his big but contentious real estate deal, into which he likely invested his last penny, became a financial disaster that left him broke? Or perhaps the family lore somehow got it all wrong. Did he not flee at all but simply die? In the end, I cannot say for certain.

TWELVE

Harry Strack, Workingman

IN LIEU OF A FATHER, Cora May Beasley, our Harry Strack's half-sister, became an important figure in the boy's life—more so than his dad ever seemed to be. May, as she was known, was 10 years older than Harry. In 1906, at age 20, she married Edward Hamernick, a 26-year-old son of Bohemian immigrants who would go on to a long career as a professional cook and restaurant manager. She gave birth to the first of their three children, a daughter named Eva May, a year after the marriage. But even as their own family was growing, the Hamernicks made room for both Harry and his mother, Mary Beasley Strack. They lived for years with May and Edward in rented apartments, following them even when Edward's career took him west to Colorado.

Later in life, Harry would tell census-takers that he had an eighth-grade education. I'm not sure that he lasted even that long in school; family lore suggests he was earning a paycheck at age 12. Harry obviously was eager to go to work—and work he did. Century-old city directories record a dizzying array of jobs that he held as a teenager and young man. The 1910 census found Harry and his mother living with the Hamernicks in an apartment in downtown Denver. Edward and May were working at a restaurant there, he as a cook and she as a cashier. Harry, at age 14, was employed as an apprentice for an awning company. His mother Mary was not working. Presumably, she cared for her toddler granddaughter, Eva May, while the parents earned a living.

A year later, the Rocky Mountain adventure was over for the Hamernick/Strack clan. In 1911, the Council Bluffs city directory showed that Harry was working as a driver—at age 15 or 16—for the Schluter Grocery Company in that city. The following year, he was living with his mother and sister's family in an apartment near the corner of Leavenworth and South 19th Streets in downtown Omaha. Edward was managing a downtown eatery called Unique Restaurant, where May was waiting tables. In 1914, Harry was working as a tinner at L.C. Thrane, a sheet-metal manufacturer in Omaha. In 1915, he was an oil company clerk. In 1916, he had moved on as a "helper" at Young & Henderson Hardware. And a year after that, he went to work as a carpet cleaner, the job he held on June 5, 1917, according to a military draft card he signed that day. Harry was described on the card as being of medium height and medium build with blue eyes and dark brown hair. The card noted that Harry was not bald—although that condition was temporary. His pate would be more shine than fuzz by the time he turned 40.

The card noted that Harry was seeking a draft deferral, claiming an exemption based on his "support of mother." It didn't work. He was drafted into the Army in time to serve out the final year of World War I. He did his minimum of two years and was discharged as a corporal. (I do not know whether he went abroad or faced combat, but his headstone at St. Mary's Cemetery in South Omaha is engraved with recognition of his military service.)

In the months just before he was drafted, Harry had changed jobs yet again—to what, by my count, was at least his seventh employer in eight years. I sense that the rapid-fire job-switching was a

Harry Strack's Draft Card

REGISTRATION CARD | No. 132

Form 3266

1. Name in full: Harry Albert Strack
2. Home address: 819 . 2. st Omaha Nebr.
3. Date of birth: July 8" 1895
4. Are you (1) a natural-born citizen, (2) a naturalized citizen, (3) an alien, (4) or have you declared your intention (specify which)? Natural Born
5. Where were you born? Council Bluffs Ia Americas
6. If not a citizen, of what country are you a citizen or subject?
7. What is your present trade, occupation, or office? Carpet Cleaner
8. By whom employed? L.J. Swift Where employed? Omaha
9. Have you a father, mother, wife, child under 12, or a sister or brother under 12, solely dependent on you for support (specify which)? Mother
10. Married or single (which)? Single Race (specify which)? Caucasian
11. What military service have you had? Rank ___ branch ___ years ___ Nation or State ___
12. Do you claim exemption from draft (specify grounds)? Support of mother

I affirm that I have verified above answers and that they are true.

Harry A Strack
(Signature of registrant)

3366

REGISTRAR'S REPORT

20-1-45-A

1. Tall, medium, or short (specify which)? Medium
2. Color of eyes? Blue Color of hair? Dark Brown Bald? No
3. Has person lost arm, leg, hand, foot, or both eyes, or is he otherwise disabled (specify)? No

I certify that my answers are true, that the person registered has read his own answers, that I have witnessed his signature, and that all of his answers of which I have knowledge are true, except as follows:

John Campbell
(Signature of registrar)

Precinct 9-2
City or County Omaha
State Neb.

July 5 '17
(Date of registration)

sign of ambition, not shiftlessness. His new job would prove to be a keeper. Sometime early in 1918, Harry walked the three blocks from his sister's downtown apartment to a smoke-belching structure that took up an entire city block at 20th and Pacific Streets. This was the Paxton-Mitchell foundry, which made its name by molding and tooling precise metal parts for steam locomotives, while also cranking out cast iron manhole covers and various types of metal grates. Omaha's 1918 city directory listed Harry Strack as a "chauffeur" for Paxton-Mitchell. I doubt this means that he was driving Mr. Paxton and Mr. Mitchell to their luncheon appointments. More likely, he was a wheelman for the company's delivery trucks. In either case, driving was a valuable skill in 1918, when America had only about 6 million motor vehicles, one for every 20 citizens. (Today, the ratio is roughly one vehicle for each of the 332 million men, women, and children in the country.)

Fresh out of the Army in 1920, Harry went back to Paxton-Mitchell—and stayed there. It was his job of a lifetime. He had also moved back in with his mother and his sister's family at 19th and Leavenworth. That year's federal census showed that the Hamernicks had grown to include three children—Eva, 13, and brothers Harold, 7, and Newton, 3. And the crowded apartment was about to get even more stuffy.

After a courtship that lasted a few months, our grandparents, Eileen Kinnear and Harry Strack, were married on October 18, 1920. He was 25, and she was 23. They were married on a Monday, so the ceremony would not have been a grand affair. The 1921 Omaha city directory listed them side by side: Eileen Strack, clerk at Rudolph Dietz, the South Omaha grocer, and Harry Strack, driver at Paxton-Mitchell. The directory showed them living at 815 South 19th Street, still with his mother and his half-sister's family of five. That means Eileen had moved out of the crowded Kinnear family home at 3014 S Street and into an even more-crowded

Hamernick-Strack apartment downtown. This living arrangement could not have lasted very long. By the end of 1921, a year after the wedding, Eileen was pregnant with her first child, Dorothy Mae, born May 22, 1922. Dorothy's middle name was a sweet homage to Harry's half-sister, who had helped shepherd her brother through a difficult childhood.

WITH THE BIRTH OF HER FIRST CHILD, Eileen was beckoned back to South Omaha. Her father had been gone for four years by then. And as Eileen's siblings grew up and moved out of the S Street house one by one, her widowed mother, Nellie, invited the newlyweds back to the homeplace. It must have been a fraught decision for Harry, moving from an apartment in the shadow of his foundry to a house that would require a long workday commute for the rest of his life. I think all of us who got to know Grandma Strack would agree that she could be quit persuasive. Harry conceded, and 3014 S Street became their home.

Nellie agreed to sell the house to Eileen and Harry, although she continued living there. As of the 1930 census, Nellie and her youngest child, Robert Kinnear, 27 years old, were both still on S Street. That census identified Harry as owner of the house, which he valued at $2,000. Over the course of the Roaring Twenties, Harry and Eileen refilled the house with their own children—four of them arriving in six years, and a fifth born after a 3½-year pause. Dorothy was followed by brother Harry Albert Jr., known as Bud, born January 2, 1924; George Edward, born December 14, 1925; Helen Marie (my mother), born March 3, 1928; and Eileen Virginia, born December 29, 1931. Eileen, the final child, shared a birthday with Bill Kinnear Sr., the grandfather she had never met. To her loved ones, Eileen was known for her entire life as Petty. She certainly was petite; even as an adult, Aunt Petty barely made five feet tall standing on tiptoes.

But her nickname came from my mother Helen's adorable toddler-talk attempt to call her little sister "pretty."

The Strack children lost both of their grandmothers 18 months apart in the mid-1930s. Harry's mother, Mary Gibler Beasley Strack, died in Omaha on June 12, 1935. She was 77 years old. A brief obituary

Harry and Eileen Strack in about 1955

in the *Omaha Bee* said she died in a hospital, although no cause was given. Harry and his half-sister, May Hamernick, were listed as survivors. Mary had continued to live with May and her family after Harry married and moved out. They were still living downtown, in an apartment building on Park Avenue, when she died. Mary Strack was buried across the river in Walnut Hill Cemetery, in the sprawling graveyard district of northeastern Council Bluffs, four miles from her family's old haunts near the railroad yards. Her body lies near the unmarked graves of her parents. Mary has a headstone, although it is inscribed with an eternal error: She was born in 1857, not 1860, as the stone states.

As Mary Strack died, Nellie Kinnear was struggling with failing heath, as well. By 1934, when the S Street house had been filled with the full complement of Strack children, Nellie had moved in with the family of her oldest daughter, Grace Kleber, at 3540 South 27th Street, around the corner from South Omaha's Highland Park. Grace's children were older than Eileen's, so I suppose she had more time and energy to care for their mother. Nellie McAuliffe Kinnear's "protracted sojourn" through life came to an end on November 24, 1936, a couple of days before Thanksgiving. A brief obituary in the *Omaha World-Herald* reported that she had died after "a lingering illness." Her death certificate, passed down to me through several generations, suggested that Nellie had been in declining health for years. Dr. William Melcher, who said he had been caring for her for a full six years, gave the cause of death as arteriosclerosis, a hardening of the arteries often attributed to smoking and a poor diet. My cousin Don Szymanski said he was told that Nellie went blind in her final years — a condition associated with blockage of retinal arteries. She also suffered from "general uremia," a chronic failure of the kidneys.

Dying at age 73, Nellie had outlived her husband by 18 years. She had spent three-quarters of her life in America, 53 years in all. Her body was laid out at 3014 S Street, following family tradition. And like her husband and deceased children, she was buried at St. Mary's Cemetery following a funeral Mass at St. Agnes. Nellie was laid to rest beside her husband, just off Q Street at the northern edge of the graveyard. I stopped by there in July 2022, while I was in Omaha for a funeral. The Kinnear plot is located in Block 4, among some of the oldest graves at St. Mary's. Their daughter, Clara Kinnear Bogatz, who died young from complications of childbirth, is buried there, as well. She is memorialized by a flat headstone. But Nellie's name does not appear on the big Woodmen of the World headstone that marks the grave of her husband. Nor is there a stone for Bill Jr., who died young of drowning. But all four are buried there, according to the brief Kinnear family history, which states, "William (Jr.) and Clara are both buried in the same plot as Ellen (Nellie) and William."

After pausing over the Kinnear graves on that hot, sunny Nebraska afternoon, I was drawn to the shade of a large tree a few dozen paces to the south. As I stood cooling off, I noticed that the tree trunk had partially engulfed a large brown headstone. I leaned down to read the inscribed names: Walter and Bridget Furlong. It was the grave of Nellie's old friend from Ireland, her traveling companion aboard the SS *Pavonia* when they emigrated in 1883. Lifelong friends, here they were, 25 yards apart in a South Omaha cemetery. It couldn't have been a coincidence that these two Irish girls wished to lie in eternal rest so close to one another that they could carry on a conversation. They had plenty to talk about: Imagine the scope of their lives, from beginnings in rural Ireland in the mid-1800s to endings in Nebraska at the doorstep of the mid-1900s.

Since they had all lived together for a number of years, the oldest of Harry and Eileen's children — Dorothy, Bud, and George — must have become well-acquainted with their Irish grandmother. Likewise, they surely were familiar with Harry's mother, Mary Strack. Even my mother, Helen, would have had some recollections from her early childhood. She would have been 8 when Nellie died. But it seems the

Bridget Murphy Furlong's Gravestone, St. Mary's Cemetery, South Omaha

Strack kids were not inclined to share these memories with their own children. Nor was their mother, Eileen, apparently. I asked my cousin Nancy Keating Walsh, who spent more time with Grandma Strack than any of us, whether she had ever spoken with her about Nellie, her mother. "No, never," Nancy said. Strange — and sad.

Despite the meager oral history in our family about Nellie, I believe that one of her characteristics lived on for several generations, even among some of the great-grandchildren that she never met. The Kinnear children, including our Grandma Strack, spoke with what linguists call an intrusive (or "epenthetic") letter R. Grandma and her siblings said *warsh* instead of wash. To them, a wash cloth was a *warsh rag.* They *warshed* the dishes, and they cleaned their clothes in the *warshing* machine. To them, our nation's capital was in *Warshington.* And if they saw a bug on the kitchen floor, they *squarshed* it under foot. My mother and her siblings inherited the *warsh* pronunciation, and they passed it along to their own children. It didn't stick with me, but my oldest siblings, Eddie and Colleen, were firmly in the *warsh and Warshington* pronunciation camp. To check that, I phoned Colleen, spelled out W-A-S-H and asked her to say the word for me. "Wash," she carefully said. After a pause, she added, "Well, *warsh*. That's how I learned to say it, and that's how I still say it." Colleen has another old-school quirk that connects her to our family's language roots. She trained her grandchildren to address her as "Bubby," from *babicka*, the Czech word for grandmother. With a laugh, Colleen told me that her pronunciation of *warsh* is a little parlor game for her granddaughter, Nadia Skradski. "Nadia will say, 'OK, Bubby, say *wash*.' And I say *warsh*, and she says, 'That's not how you're supposed to say it!' And I tell her, 'Well, that's how I say it!'" Colleen told me that years ago, a relative who did not come from our Strack line tried to correct her pronunciation. "She told me, 'Don't call it a *warsh rag*. Call it a *face cloth*.'" The attempted fix failed. Colleen still calls it a *warsh rag*, with a little touch of stubborn South Omaha pride.

The pronunciation is not random, Nadia. This lingual peculiarity, known as the Midland dialect, is fading today, dying out with your Bubby's generation. But it once was common in certain locales across a wide swath of the Midwest, including in our South Omaha family. Its origins are obscure, but language experts say that Colleen's *warsh* pronunciation was most commonly found in families, neighborhoods, or regions with deep Scots-Irish connections. Linguists say *warsh* is "transmitted" from one generation to the next, and our family serves as proof of that. So for the Kinnear-Strack-Krajicek line (and many of our cousins of a certain age), *warsh* was a linguistic gift from our great-grandparents, William and Nellie Kinnear—he from Scotland, she from Ireland.

THIRTEEN

New Generations

REPLENISHED WITH CHILDREN, 3014 S Street became my family's hub for another generation. Harry and Eileen Strack decided to educate their children not at St. Agnes, the old Kinnear religious homebase, but at St. Anthony Catholic Church, just a few minutes by foot up S Street. This was an interesting choice, no doubt made by Eileen. Typical of American big cities, most of South Omaha's Catholic churches had an immigrant ethnic identity—St. Stanislaus was Polish, Our Lady of Guadalupe was Mexican, Assumption was Czech, St. Frances Cabrini was Italian, and so forth. St. Anthony's was home to South Omaha's large Lithuanian immigrant population. Now remember that Eileen was the daughter of an Irish mother, and St. Mary's, a church and grade school with a largely Irish congregation, was just a few blocks beyond St. Anthony's. Yet I recall Grandma saying that she didn't want to have anything to do with St. Mary's—too many Irish! On the other hand, she seemed to loved Lithuanians. As my cousin Nancy Walsh Keating told me, "When my sister Mary Beth married Bob Naujokaitis, my mom told me that Grandma would be very happy: She finally got a Lithuanian in the family!"

Many of Grandma Strack's closest friends were Lithuanian. I'm certain our outspoken grandmother had her reasons for favoring the Lithuanian St. Anthony's over the Irish St. Mary's—and she would have told any of us who had the foresight to ask. But that's now another unanswerable question in our family's story. Whatever her motivation, Eileen saw to it that her children grew up at St. Anthony's. Just imagine what their mother's educational decision would have meant to her kids—her Scottish/Irish/German kids. Even by the standards of the ethnic Balkanization of Catholic parishes in Omaha, St. Anthony's had a particularly strong identity as Lithuanian. Founded in 1906, it was said to be the only Lithuanian Catholic parish west of the Mississippi River. By tradition, its pastor was Lithuanian, and for many of them English was a second language. Over the years, St. Anthony's pastors included Father Zarkauskas, Father Musteikis, Father Jonaitis, Father Krasnickas— names straight out of Vilnius, Kaunas, or any other Lithuanian city.

The congregation felt very strongly about its ethnic identity, according to a remarkable profile of the parish published in *Nebraska History* in 2003 by historian Jonathan P. Herzog. "St. Anthony's was more than a physical building," Herzog wrote. "The church on 32nd Street was the lifeblood of the Lithuanian community, providing immigrants with an indispensable network of material, social, and cultural support." His article dug down deeply into an interesting ethnic controversy that erupted there in the early 1930s, as the older Strack kids were beginning grade school at St. Anthony's. Lithuanian parishioners had revolted against the pastor, George Mikulskis, fearing that St. Anthony's was losing its "cultural homogeneity," according to Herzog. The problem? Despite his Lithuanian surname and a conversational understanding of that language, Father Mikulskis was half-Polish, and he preached in English. For many longtime parishioners, he was deemed insufficiently Lithuanian. As a group of prominent women church members wrote to the local bishop, "As there are many of us who cannot understand the English language, we leave the services with tears in our eyes, for we did not understand the sermons." The conflict dragged on for several years before the Lithuanian bloc finally ran off Mikulskis in 1932. "It is impossible for me to stay any longer," the priest wrote. He was replaced by a new pastor, Father Joseph Jusevich, a native of Kalesninkas, Lithuania, whose ethnic purity passed muster with the congregation. Soon, St. Anthony's ran off its non-ethnic Ursuline order of nuns, as well, replacing them with the Sisters of Casimir, a religious order based in Chicago but rooted in the Lithuanian village of Ramygala. Father Jusevich reported that a parish poll found that 147 of the 149 families of St. Anthony's preferred the Casimirs over the Ursulines. (I wonder if the Strack family was one of the two outliers?) Although most were born in the United States, Casimir nuns were expected to understand the Lithuanian language. Even today, the order declares, "From the birth of our Foundress in Ramygala, Lithuania, through to the present day, we honor and maintain our ties to Lithuania."

This wave of Lithuanian nationalism at St. Anthony's was cresting at about the time my mother arrived for her first day of school in 1934, the year after the Sisters of Casimir were placed in charge. She would have been greeted by a nun in full habit, showing only a small window of skin from chin to eyebrow and cheek to cheek. My mother and her siblings must have felt as though they were being transported back to Ramygala to learn their ABCs. They weren't the only non-Lithuanians who attended school there in the 1930s and '40s, but they were part of a small minority. Records show that extracurricular activities at St. Anthony's in that era included Lithuanian movies, Lithuanian guest speakers, meetings of the Lithuanian Language Club, and special productions by the parish's own Lithuanian Folk Dance Group and Lithuanian Drama Club.

What a surreal trip through grade school it must have been for a family of Scots-Irish kids who just happened to live down the block.

THE STRACK KIDS GREW UP as South Omaha, like the rest of the nation, was in the clutches of the Great Depression. My mother, Helen, was born 19 months before the stock market crash of October 29, 1929, that raised the curtain on one of America's most devastating economic eras. The Depression dragged on for a full 10 years, and the Strack family surely felt its effects. But if my mother and her siblings were deprived of basic necessities, she did not share those stories with us. I do know that Harry, Eileen, and their kids maintained a large vegetable garden in the backyard, on soil originally cultivated decades before by Bill and Nellie Kinnear. Grandma Eileen grew up eating produce from that fertile plot, and so did her children. Like many women of the era, Eileen was a talented seamstress—no doubt taught by her own mother. She spent hours each week at her sewing machine, turning out all types of clothing for her kids, from dresses to dungarees. "My mom said Grandma made everything they wore," my cousin Nancy Keating Walsh told me. The clothes were handed down through the family—from Dorothy to Helen to Petty, and from Bud to George.

Eileen did not work outside the home after her babies began to arrive, so Harry must have felt pressure to provide for his family. And he did so. Records show that he managed to keep his job at the foundry throughout the 1930s, even during the grimmest years of the Depression. In the 1940 Census, Harry reported that he had been fully employed for the previous 12 months, earning $1,200 in that period. That means he was supporting his wife and five children on a salary of a hundred bucks a month, $23 a week. Yet they apparently were relatively well-off, by one federal standard. Census-takers in

The Strack teenagers with their parents in about 1945:
Helen, Dorothy, George, and Petty. Brother Harry is missing.

1940 were required to ask each household a question designed to indicate degree of wealth: Do you own a radio? The Stracks reported that they had a radio—one of just three houses on their block that enjoyed such an extravagance.

Harry's weekly pay envelope may not have been particularly heavy, but he was a model of consistent employment—a true company man. He was listed as a Paxton-Mitchell employee in Omaha's R.L. Polk City Directory for a full 40 years, from 1918 until 1958. He held a number of positions, and the city directories reveal the arc of his career. He began as a "chauffer" in 1918 and stayed behind the wheel for two decades as a truck driver, delivering Paxton-Mitchell's industrial steel products to local customers. By 1940, at age 45, Harry stepped down from his truck to work as a shipping clerk, overseeing the preparation and delivery of orders; today, we'd call him a logistics specialist. He must have done his job well: In the late 1940s and into the early '50s, he was listed in the city directory as a foreman or supervisor. And as retirement age approached, it seems that Paxton-Mitchell found lower-stress jobs that kept the paychecks coming for his final four or five years as a workingman. He spent a couple of years as a carpenter there, probably building shipping containers for metal products, and then retired as a maintenance man in about 1960, at age 65.

My cousin Mary Dundis Lincoln, daughter of Dorothy Strack Dundis, told me that she and her sister Susan spent a week every summer at the South Omaha home of our Strack grandparents. She said Harry's arrival each afternoon was a relief from long days with our sometimes prickly grandmother. "I remember looking forward to Grandpa coming home after work carrying his black lunch pail," Mary said. Diplomatically, she added, "He was a mild-tempered man compared to Grandma."

Harry must have worn out more than a few of those lunch buckets. Over his four decades at Paxton-Mitchell, Eileen sent him off each and every working day with a homemade lunch—some 10,000 meals in all, by my count. As their children grew up and joined the work force, her lunch prep must have resembled an assembly line. In the late '40s, while Harry was a supervisor at Paxton Mitchell, he finagled positions there for his two sons, Bud and George, after they had finished wartime stints in the U.S. Navy. And their younger sister, my mother Helen, joined the Strack family carpool for a year or two. After finishing up at Omaha South High School, she worked in downtown Omaha on the coffee packaging line at Paxton & Gallagher, a wholesale grocery merchant. For a year or two, there must have been a four-Strack South Omaha carpool to and from downtown—Harry, Bud, George, and Helen.

The Strack boys mustn't have been as enthralled with the foundry work as their father. Each moved on after a couple of years under Harry's wing. George went to work in the packinghouses, including many years at Wilson & Company. Bud worked for the Union Pacific Railroad for a few years, then had a long career as a heavy equipment operator for the City of Omaha. My mother moved on, too, giving up the aroma of coffee for a job at the local phone company, Northwestern Bell, before marriage and motherhood interceded.

AFTER PERSEVERING THROUGH their Lithuanian grade school experience, the Strack kids all attended South High School, on South 24th Street about a mile from home. (The school's nickname pays homage to South Omaha's predominant industry: the Packers.) Adulthood came quickly for all five Stracks; each married young. Fresh out of the service at age 22, George Strack married Alice Volcek, 19, in April 1948. His brother, Bud, married a South Omaha Czech, Helen Vodicka, in 1947.

My parents, Helen Strack and Edward L. Krajicek, were high school sweethearts at South High. My father washed out of college after a semester at Creighton University, then joined the Navy as a Plan B as World War II was ending. After two torturously boring years in the service, much it spent working in the pharmacy of a mostly empty military hospital in Hawaii, he returned to Omaha and married Helen on June 18, 1949.

My mother's kid sister, Petty, found her one-and-only at a dance at Omaha's Sokol Auditorium, according to her daughter, Nancy Keating Walsh. Petty's beau, Nicholas Joseph Keating, known as Joe, grew up in South Omaha's Irish Hill neighborhood, the son of an Irish immigrant father. (Mary Beth Keating pointed out to me that while everyone knew their mother as Petty—from my mother's toddler attempt to call her "pretty"—Joe always called her by her birth name, Eileen. "Dad never called her Petty," Mary Beth said.) They were married on August 1, 1953.

I am lucky enough to know how Dorothy, the oldest Strack child, met her future husband, our Uncle Al, Alphonse C. Dundis. Al and Dorothy were the parents of five children, all daughters—Judy, Mary, Susan, Barb and Terri. As my career as a newspaperman and journalism professor took root in New York City, Al and I developed an affinity and friendship. He was an intelligent, well-educated man who followed current events closely. He was an avid reader of newspapers and was always curious about my work and, more broadly, how the media business operated. As he got older, I made a point of trying to visit with Uncle Al each time I returned home to Omaha.

In about 2010, at nearly 90 years old, Al had taken a fall and was convalescing at Methodist Hospital in Omaha. I happened to be in town, so I went to see him one evening. He was alone in his room, just finishing up a hospital dinner when I arrived. He greeted me warmly, but he certainly wasn't the smiling, jocular gentleman I had always known. His beloved wife had died about a year before, and he was depressed—still aching over the loss. When I asked how he was doing, Al told me firmly and with misty eyes that he was ready to die so he could be reunited with Dorothy, the love of his life.

I tried to finesse the conversation away from his loss. I knew that Al had had a long career as a manager at Mutual of Omaha, the giant insurance company, but I knew little of his origin story. So I asked him to tell me about his childhood. Without flinching, Al told me he was raised in poverty after his father abandoned his mother. He told me they lived in one of South Omaha's Polish neighborhoods, near St. Stanislaus Church. He said he owed his success in life to his mother and to a St. Stan's priest who took an interest in his education. He said the priest personally arranged a scholarship for him at both Creighton Prep, an elite, all-boys Catholic high school, and Creighton University.

I then asked how he had met my Aunt Dorothy, and his demeanor changed completely. He softened, turned toward me, fully engaged, and told the story. It was during World War II—in 1939 or 1940. I believe Al said he was a college freshman, so he would have been about 19 years old. He said he was working an after-school job in the mid-afternoon at the *Omaha World-Herald's* South Omaha circulation office, located just off the main drag of South 24th Street. Newspaper trucks would rumble up at 3 or 3:30 with bundles of the freshly printed evening edition, which Al and his young colleagues sorted and distributed to local paperboys or drivers who dropped bundles at spots around South Omaha. Al's job, as a circulation supervisor, was to make sure that the proper number of papers got to the right places.

One day, Al told me, he noticed a beautiful young brunette walk by on South 24th Street. She was carrying schoolbooks, and he reckoned that she was a student walking home from nearby South

High. Al saw her pass again a few days later. Captivated, he began making a point of watching for her each weekday afternoon. He told me that he grew so distracted anticipating her passage that he worried his boss would fire him.

After many days of what he thought was secret admiration, Al said, he noticed that the girl was casting shy glances back at him. One day, Al remarked about the girl's stunning beauty to another teenager—also a South High student—who worked with him divvying up newspaper bundles.

The guy shrugged.

Al asked whether he knew the girl.

"Sure," he said. "She's my sister."

Al asked, "Does she go with anyone?"

"Nope," said the boy.

And then Al told me that he asked the boy this heart-melting question: "Do I stand a chance with her?"

The boy was Bud Strack, and the girl was his older sister, Dorothy. It turned out that Al did stand a chance. Bud introduced the two a few days later. They soon were a couple, embarking on a life together that spanned some 70 years. Al had tears in his eyes— happy tears—as he finished his little story. So did I.

BY THE TIME THEIR CHILDREN had finished procreating, Harry and Eileen Strack were grandparents more than 30 times over. The youngest, Petty, had seven children. My mother, Helen, had eight. Dorothy had the five daughters. George had seven kids with two wives. Bud and his wife, Helen, were the outliers, with *just* four children. As I was doing the math to add up this long list of grandchildren, I could almost understand why Grandma used to toss water in our faces through her screen door to keep us locked outside during S Street get-togethers.

Dorothy Strack and her little sister Eileen (Petty) in about 1942

The Keating and Krajicek cousins were particularly close, not surprising since our mothers, Helen and Petty, were closest in age and fast friends who lived near one another. My cousin Nancy Keating Walsh recalls that our mothers would haul their ever-growing tribes to Grandma Strack's house every Saturday. (This must have been quite a logistical feat since none of the Strack girls, Dorothy, Helen, or Petty, ever learned to drive a car.) I remember Saturday night card games there, with the Strack siblings and their spouses playing 31, a rollicking variation on Blackjack that—from my memory—involved drawing and discarding cards until someone "knocked," which always prompted frolic. I seem to recall that Grandma Strack was particularly adept—and my mother not so much. Interestingly, I have learned that 31 has been popular for centuries in England and Ireland. I wonder if Nellie introduced her children (and grandchildren) to the game?

My older siblings, Eddie, Colleen, and Ricky, were pals with Uncle George Strack's older boys from his first marriage, George Jr., Kerrie, Bobby Joe, and Wesley. Several of the boys were farmed out to the homes of cousins when George's marriage faltered. Kerrie lived with us on Polk Street for a few months. While checking that recollection with my sister Colleen, she told me a cute story involving cousin Kerrie:

I guess we got mad because Dad was going down to Darby's Tavern and leaving us at home. One day, we decided we weren't going to take that shit anymore. So what did we do? Ricky, Kerrie, and me packed up a little bag and ran away from home. The first thing we did was stop at Sts. Peter and Paul Church and said a prayer. [She laughed and slapped her knee.] *Then we walked down two blocks to Grandpa Krajicek's house and sat in his little green trailer for a while. An hour later, we said, "Hey, we better get back home! What's gonna happen when it gets dark!"*

By the early 1960s, the Strack family began to grow more dispersed. Kerrie's mother, Alice, moved to Mississippi with her sons, and we rarely saw the Strack boys after that. (Uncle George Strack remarried in the mid-1960s, and he and his wife Katherine had two children, Tim and Kim.) George's older brother and his wife, Bud and Helen, raised their four children in South Omaha's Brown Park neighborhood. As Al and Dorothy Dundis's family grew, they left South Omaha and settled in Omaha's Benson section, 10 miles across the city from S Street. They lived five or six blocks from downtown Benson and were longtime members of the nearby St. Bernard's Catholic Church. Dorothy and Al worked to maintain close family contact, despite the distance. They always attended important family event—birthdays, graduations, weddings. I asked my cousin Mary Dundis Lincoln about her recollections of our grandparents, and she told me that she and her sisters had a different relationship than some of us:

The Dundis girls do not have the same memories of Grandma and Grandpa as the rest of you do. We lived so far away from them so didn't have the daily interaction as those of you that lived close. I remember that we used to pile in the car after dinner on Sunday and drive to Grandma and Grandpa's for a visit. We always looked forward to it. Grandpa sat in his chair next to his ash tray and smoked like a fiend. I do remember holidays when their house buzzed with lots of kids running around. With the Keatings, your siblings, and the five of us, it was a house full.

For years Sue and I spent a week with them in the summer. I remember walking to the grocery store at least once a day to buy food for the day. We would walk to downtown South Omaha with her, walking by the packing-house. We would buy very little but we did buy the yarn to make hot pads. Sue and I had to sleep upstairs, and we were scared to death, but she would just tell us to go to sleep.

That is another fine anecdote to describe our Grandma Strack. Her grandmotherly comfort for the frightened little ones: "Just go to sleep!" My father would have applied one of his signature descriptions to Grandma Strack: "She was a different bird." Worried that I was being too shrill in this portrait of my mother's mother, I checked my biases by asking a number of my siblings and cousins for their impressions of Grandma Strack. When I put the question to my youngest Keating cousin, Mary Beth, she replied without a moment's pause: "She scared the hell out of me." My younger sister Carol offered a one-word summary of our grandmother: "Mean."

In the 1970s, a year or so before Grandma Strack died, she was visiting our house on Polk Street for some occasion. Like many teenagers, my cousin Nick Keating and I had grown our hair out. Nick had a fabulous, foot-wide, rust-colored Afro, and I had thick brown hair that went on forever. We walked into the living room together to say hello to Grandma, and she just about fell off her chair. "Oh, my God," she hooted. "If it ain't Jesus and Moses come to life." (I think I was Jesus and Nick was Moses.) Did I mention that she had a sense of humor?

AS THE ST. ANTHONY'S "cultural homogeneity" flap showed, ethnic identity has always been an issue of consequence in South Omaha. I certainly felt that, growing up with an unusual surname — bookended by the letter K — that even white-bread strangers are generally able to identify as eastern European. The name is Czech — or Bohemian, as my grandfather, Edward F. Krajicek, would more likely say. Both of his parents, Vaclav Krajicek and Anna Kopecka, were immigrants from Bohemia, and Czech was my Grandpa Krajicek's first language. When I was a teenager, Grandpa Krajicek frequently encouraged me to find a nice Bohemian-American girl to marry. Just as often, he warned me against hooking up with Irish girls — "little devils," he would call them.

Ah, but my own dear mother's grandmother was from Ireland, so I guess it's complicated, isn't it? Two generations along, my surname brands me as Czech, and I doubled down on that identity by studying the language and living in Prague during the 1990s while directing a journalism program at Charles University there. But how Czech am I? An analysis of my DNA shows that my national origins are pan-European. But my ancestral profile says that my genetics are 55 percent Great Britain and Ireland and just 20 percent Czech. This doesn't change who I am, but it certainly colors my ethnic self-identity. So has this book project. With what I have learned, I can now stand in the places in Ireland and Scotland where my maternal great-grandparents took their first steps.

Grandma Strack always identified as "Scots-Irish," even though she spent three-quarters of her life carrying her husband's very Germanic surname. German identity became a mark of shame after that country's atrocities of World War II, and Grandma apparently decided to scrub her husband's German roots. This was revealed in a testy bit of conversation at a family gathering between Strack sisters Dorothy Dundis and Petty Keating late in their lives, witnessed by several members of the Keating family. Dorothy mentioned the Strack family's German roots, and Petty curtly replied, "Ma always said not to talk about that." Dorothy shot back, "Well, Ma's dead now, so what."

 I HAD MANY CONVERSATIONS about our shared family history with my cousin Nancy Keating Walsh, Aunt Petty's oldest child. As I said, Nancy had a close relationship with Grandma Strack; she says they bonded when she was an infant, after she was

entrusted to Grandma's care for several months when Petty broke an elbow in a car wreck. Nancy was a kind and caring granddaughter who returned that favor by looking after Grandma in her final years. I asked her about Grandma's reputation.

"I know some of our cousins believe Grandma Strack had a mean streak, but she was never mean to me," Nancy said. "I think she was a product of her nationality, Scottish and Irish. My Grandma Keating was the same way—she had a biting tongue. She was going to tell you what was on her mind, regardless of what you thought about it."

My oldest sister, Colleen Krajicek, also has fonder memories of our grandmother than some of us. "I think she was from a generation when people didn't look at their grandkids the same way we do today," Colleen told me. "First of all, I think everyone was overwhelmed with the number of kids. All of her children had big families, and all these kids would descend on her house at the same time . . . Who could stand to have so many kids running around all at once, and we ran around like crazy, didn't we?"

Yes, we did. My siblings and I had an unmarried paternal great-aunt, Rose Krajicek, who came to our house for holiday meals several times a year. She had a different way of dealing with the mayhem. She would smile tightly and sip a whiskey Presbyterian, eat, then promptly shove off for home. After she died, I was given a few letters that Rose had written to another relative. "Well, I spent another Christmas with the orangutans," our dear Auntie Rose wrote. My siblings and I were the orangutans. (And we thought she liked us.) This was her way of dealing with unruly kids—smile to our faces, then bang out her complaints on a typewriter.

That was not Eileen Strack's modus operandi. Nancy and Colleen are right that Grandma Strack was a straight-shooter, and part of that might be cultural or generational. She also lacked sensitivity, which might be a positive trait. Her son George was cut from the same piece of Scots-Irish wool. He had a mean streak, and he was a relentless teaser. I was a chubby kid, and my Uncle George Strack nicknamed me "hog jowls." I hated it, and he knew it, which led him to bully me even more. I screamed at him, I attacked him, I cussed him — all of which seemed to delight George. It still puzzles me that a 40-something uncle would bully an 8-year-old boy. Not to make excuses for him, but George's behavior may have been related to a serious drinking problem that he struggled with in his 30s and 40s. His drinking often landed him in the local papers. I searched the *Omaha World-Herald* archives and found George Strack's name about a dozen times in the early 1960s for drinking-related driving infractions — drunken driving, reckless driving, careless driving, negligent driving, failure to yield. He was hell on wheels, apparently. To his credit, Uncle George got a grip on his drinking before it killed him — or someone else.

One other anecdote about teasing, this one more loving: I was an inquisitive kid — a nice way of admitting that I was a pain in the butt. I had a lot of questions, and I wanted answers. (That hasn't changed.) I would follow my mom around the house, badgering her, and she figured out a way to badger me back, in good humor. I don't recall my precise question, but I wanted to know how, when, or why she had obtained one household object or another. After I asked six or eight times, she replied, "I stole eggs and bought it." I asked again and got the same reply: "Stole eggs and bought it." This probably was a stroke of mothering genius. It shut me up for a bit because my 4-year-old brain could not deduce what the hell those five words meant. *Stole eggs and what?* She would not relent to explain, so her answer became a running tease that went on for months — another way of saying, "Oh, shut up, kid."

Within a couple of years, we would lose our mother, and *Stole eggs and bought it* became one of the enduring mysteries of my brief time with her. I've been unable to find any reference to the phrase —

in print or online—and, trust me, I've tried. In 2013, I visited my Aunt Petty Keating at a nursing home a few months before she died. While we were chatting about her memories of my mother, a light bulb went off.

"Aunt Petty," I said, "are you familiar with the phrase '*Stole eggs and bought it*'? My mom used to say that to me when I asked too many questions."

"Oh, sure," she told me. "That was one of Ma's [*Grandma Strack's*] sayings. She got it from her."

My heart skipped a beat, my pulse quickened. At long last, the answer was at hand. I leaned in close.

"So what does it mean," I whispered.

"I have no idea," Petty said. "Just some old nonsense."

Such teases, those Stracks.

FOURTEEN

A Mom's Life

IN THE MID-1950s, Petty Keating and her husband, our Uncle Joe, were early adopters of the home-movies fad. At holiday gatherings, Joe would light up the room with his Bell and Howell camera rig and record moving pictures of the extended Strack family's hijinks. Among other things, Uncle Joe's movies documented a charming tradition that Grandma Strack apparently started. After church on Easter Sunday, she organized a little Easter Parade in the backyard. Children and adults alike, all wearing their Easter best, would line up near the garage and strut in all their finery toward Uncle Joe's Bell and Howell. In another of these old films, Eileen and Harry Strack sit and laugh gleefully as their three oldest Krajicek grandchildren, Eddie, Colleen, and Ricky, turn somersaults atop one another in the front room on S Street. These long-forgotten treasures were found in a closet by my Keating cousins after Aunt Petty died. They shared them with me, and I sat stunned as I watched moving-picture glimpses of my mother, Helen, as a happy and healthy young woman, bringing her to life in a way that old still photos never could. Yet to my eyes, the soundless films have a melancholy edge — images of a time and place that have been lost.

All families have their trials, I suppose, and ours has had its share. In Grandma Strack's younger days, she suffered through the drowning of her oldest sibling, Billy Kinnear, in 1911 and the death of her sister, Clara, from complications of childbirth in 1928. My father told me several times that every parent must be prepared for heartbreak. "The decision of how many children you have is also a question of how much heartbreak you can take," he said. By a combination of chance and choice, I fathered no children of my own. Perhaps my subconscious was shielding my heart.

In 1959, Joe and Petty Keating suffered a tragedy when their third child, a toddler named Tommy, accidentally entangled himself in a curtain pull and died of strangulation. "That was a pain that my mother never got over," Nancy Keating Walsh told me. "She told me, 'You don't get over it. You just learn to live with it.'" The mode of death added a layer of guilt, Nancy said. "It was an accident, but I'm sure she still felt guilty. Any parent would."

Five years later, hearts were cleaved again in our family. After their marriage in 1949, my parents, Ed and Helen Krajicek, drove to the Rocky Mountains for a honeymoon, then returned home to Omaha, moved into 3014 S Street with her parents, and got right to work building a family. In July 1950, a month before the birth of their first child, Eddie Jr., the couple borrowed $2,500 from Uncle Frank (Darby) Krajicek to buy a building lot at 3901 Polk Street in South Omaha. They paid to have a cinder-block basement constructed there and lived in five rooms below-ground for a couple of years, in what was known in South Omaha as a flattop. Their first three children, Eddie, Colleen, and Ricky, arrived exactly 12 months apart in August 1950, 1951, and 1952. Construction of the above-ground portion of the three-bedroom house began during Helen's pregnancy with me, in 1955. They filled those bedrooms quickly. Sister Carol arrived in 1957 and Julie in '60. Julie's birth completed a busy decade of mothering for Helen—six children in just under 10 years. My dad liked to say, "People thought I was a sex fiend, but she got pregnant just about every time we did it."

My mother seemed to be a well-tuned breeding machine. For a decade, childbirth came easily and without apparent complications for her. On the evening of September 24, 1962, our hugely pregnant mother stood in the front room at 3901 Polk and said goodbye to her six children. She was off to give birth again — twins, this time. There were smiles, hugs, and kisses. Little Julie, a toddler of 2 with eyes full of tears, grabbed hold of mom's maternity smock and would not let go. The older kids pried her hands away. After more embraces, our mother walked out the door wearing what I remember as a glum smile. The next time we saw her, a few days later, she was in a casket. Before the public wake began, we children were ushered into a room at Larkin's Funeral Home in South Omaha. We were kept at a distance, perhaps 30 feet away, in a space lined with chairs but otherwise empty. Even from so far, I could see her pale white face and black hair. She was outfitted in a deep blue dress — to me, still the color of death. She was just 34 years old.

Pregnant with twin daughters, her severe anemia had gone undiagnosed by an obstetrician who missed the telltale symptoms of fatigue, headaches, and dizziness. I'm no doctor, but I can see from photos of my mother taken late that summer that she was in distress. The anemia was robbing her of the healthy red blood cells that carry life-sustaining oxygen to vital organs. Anemia is not uncommon among women pregnant with twins, and the condition could have been easily treated with iron, vitamin supplements, and bed rest — if only the doctor had done his job.

Every death can be a tragedy, some more so than others. Maternal mortality, in which a woman loses her life in service to procreation, surely qualifies. According to the U.S. Department of Health, the maternal mortality rate in 1962 for pregnant white women in the United States was about 24 deaths per 100,000 live

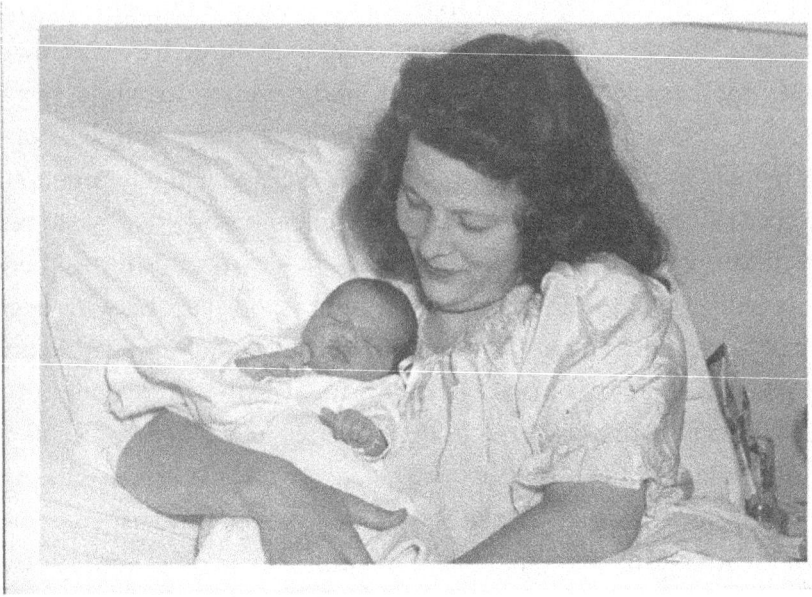

Helen Strack Krajicek

births — one mother lost for every 4,167 children born. Today, the death rate for white mothers has declined to about 15 deaths per 100,000 births — still too high. And the parallel statistics for Black women ought to concern all of us: in 1962, the mortality rate for minority moms was four times that of white women, one death for every 1,000 births, and it continues to be much higher today, at roughly triple that of white maternal mortality. As with the death of my mother, survival hinges on competent, attentive health care — something often lacking in poor communities.

Nowadays, the medical profession is keenly focused on what it calls "preventable errors," certainly more so than in 1962. "There is no greater tragedy within a medical center than when a patient dies due to a preventable error," according to the Virginia Mason Institute, a Seattle-based nonprofit focused on eliminating avoidable death and injury in healthcare. The institute estimates that nearly

100,000 Americans die each year from preventable medical errors of all types. I thought of my mother recently when I read a magazine article by Dr. Jerome Groopman, a highly respected cancer specialist who writes with great clarity about his occupation. In the piece, Groopman described the "fundamental struggle" of the medical profession: "balancing the ego required to take responsibility for another person's life with the humility to acknowledge our capacity for catastrophic error."

Over the years, I spoke with my father a few times about the circumstances of Helen's death. He told me he regretted the rapid-fire pregnancies. He cast some blame on the Catholic church and its stated mission of abundant procreation, the health of mothers be damned. But he also acknowledged that everyone was too lackadaisical about the physical risks to my mother after the first six births seemed so easy. And by *everyone*, he included himself.

 I AM NOT BEING FLIPPANT when I refer to my mother as a breeding machine. Sadly, that was the context of her entire adult life. I have taken a closer look at the social-sexual dynamics of 1962 as I try to understand, all these years later, how our mother ended up perishing in service to the creation of children. I'd like to share a few of my thoughts, which have been ricocheting around my brain for years.

The issue extends far beyond her inattentive doctor. Helen and many women of her generation gave themselves over to motherhood and housewifery. I do wonder how differently her life might have turned out had she been born 25 years later. As my mother died, much of the western world was reexamining assumptions about the role of women. In 1960, Enovid, the first oral contraceptive, went on sale in America. Millions of women soon were using "the pill," and personal autonomy on issues of reproduction became a hallmark of the women's equality movement in the 1960s. Six months after Helen's death, Betty Friedan published her feminist manifesto, *The Feminine Mystique*, which challenged the idea that women (like Helen) could feel thoroughly fulfilled as housewives consumed by childcare.

By the time I came of age in the 1970s, many of the young woman I knew were reading *Our Bodies, Ourselves*, the bible of the feminist women's health movement, whose keystones were reproductive rights and sexual awareness. Many of these friends were on the pill. By and large, these were church-going Catholics—which points up a troubling disconnect between the unmarried (and, at least theoretically, celibate) men who rule Catholicism and its more than 1 billion worldwide adherents, most of whom are sexually active, whether married or not.

The pill freaked out the Catholic Church. In 1968, Pope Paul VI was compelled to weigh in on the use of oral contraceptives in his *Humanae Vitae* (Of Human Life), an encyclical letter "on the regulation of birth." I found a copy on the Vatican's website. It's a remarkable document, seemingly more Medieval than Swingin' Sixties. The pope decreed, "The Church . . . teaches that each and every marital act must of necessity retain its intrinsic relationship to the procreation of human life." By "marital act," he meant sex.

Whew. No pressure.

He went on to suggest that sterilization or abortion would lead to certain damnation. The pope's decree further forbade "any action which either before, at the moment of, or after sexual intercourse, is specifically intended to prevent procreation." That means the use of condoms, diaphragms, and the pill were verboten, as well.

My parents were typical practicing Catholics of their generation—church on Sunday, a prayer recited by rote before meals. But they were not particularly religious. If my mother had any sense, and I believe she did, I think that she might have used contraception herself had she survived beyond eight children. In a 1992 U.S. Supreme Court ruling that reaffirmed a woman's rights concerning childbirth — before the Catholic majority now dominating the court reversed 50 years of legal precedent — the justices noted that "the ability of women to participate equally in the economic and social life of the nation has been facilitated by their ability to control their reproductive lives." Again, those words prompt thoughts of my mother. Was she able to "participate equally" in life, amid her serial pregnancies? I'm afraid she was not.

I would love to ask my mother for her perspective on all of this — if only I could. On her behalf, I want to add a note of personal grievance. As those who know me are aware, I resent Catholicism. I have many reasons, including the fact that my parish priest in the 1960s, a man whose importance in my life as an adolescent was second only to my own father, turned out to be one of the thousands of sexual predators among the Catholic clergy. (He did not molest me.) I deplore the self-serving Catholic hierarchy that hid these atrocities for generations. But my resentment is also rooted in the failures of the church after my mother died. As I see it, she lost her life in service to the pope's edict of uninhibited procreation. But what did the church do for her children, those of us she created? Here is my account.

On the second morning after our mother left us to give birth that final time, the six of us were trooped up Polk Street to the home of her friend Dee Brinjak, where a priest was waiting to break the news to us. Inside Dee's house, I caught a glimpse of my dad sitting at the kitchen table, smoking a cigarette with a wildly trembling hand. What was he doing there? We knew something was up. We were briefly quarantined in the TV room. Soon, the three older kids, Eddie, Colleen, and Ricky — aged 12, 11, and 10 — were led upstairs to a bedroom, where a priest named Dorsey (not the molester) told them that our mother had died. I still can hear Ricky's wails. They were led back down, then it was my turn to go upstairs and face Dorsey with my younger sisters, Carol and Julie. We were 6, 5, and 2. I don't remember a thing Dorsey said. After he finished talking, I made my way to the Brinjaks' basement and concealed myself behind a refrigerator. I stood there for a long time, maybe hours, alone with this fresh, gaping wound to my heart.

Those few words from Dorsey amounted to the only conversation I ever had with anyone from my church—and its affiliated grade school, which we all attended for eight years—about the death of our mother. As I reached adulthood, I came up with a pat response anytime the subject of her early death came up: *I feel sorry for her loss, not for my own.* But while I was in therapy 20 years ago, trying to sort out my failings in personal relationships, a psychologist quickly linked my issues with trust, love, and commitment to the loss of my mother at age 6. The therapist, whom I visited five or six times, was surprised that this was a revelation to me. She asked whether professional counseling or therapy had been provided to me and my siblings—from my city's social welfare agency, from my father's job, and so forth.

"None," I replied. "We weren't therapy kind of people."

"Well, you should have been," she said. "Therapy was created to help people just like you find their way through tragedies just like this."

She then asked about faith-based counseling through our church. I told her that, beyond the two minutes with Dorsey, I had never been approached by any cleric, whether priest, brother, or nun, during my many years attending Catholic church and schools. Two decades later, I recall her words distinctly: "What's the purpose of a church if it has no mechanism to help its members through a cataclysm like this? It should have been a top priority, for both your father and his children."

She was right, of course. And as I see it now, the church was hell-bent on its official mission of procreation but had nothing to offer when that mission had an inconvenient outcome. Everyone seemed to think it was better for all of us if the subject was buried with our mother. The first misstep in this process of quick erasure was the strange decision to keep her children at a distance from her casket. We should have been allowed to weep over our mother's remains. But we were kept at bay — physically and emotionally. This set a tone for our lives. After we lost our mother, we didn't talk about her. Even well into adulthood, I convinced myself that our shared grief was best left mute — one of those "thoughts that . . . lie too deep for tears," as the poet William Wordsworth wrote. I was wrong. Each of Helen's children have gone through periods of sizzling rage and/or deep melancholy, and none of us was offered the counseling that might have helped make sense of our perplexing loss and how it would affect our lives and relationships — forever.

I hope that this history of our mother and her people helps reconcile that mistake by filling in our gauzy image of who she was — a funny, bright, vibrant, beautiful woman. My cousin Nancy Keating Walsh told me, "Your mother was my mother's best friend. She told me that she missed her every day of her life." So have I — so have we all, in ways that we're still trying to understand, 60 years later. I have come to regard her death not only as a tragedy, but as a heroic act — an astounding accomplishment. As her organs were shutting down from the anemia, two healthy babies were removed from her womb — our sisters Helen and Marie, named for their mother. It has always pained me that the lives of these two innocent participants must always be associated with their mother's demise. Their birthday, after all, was the day that we all lost her. That has been a heavy burden for them to carry. Today, both of the twins have their own children and grandchildren — each a living tribute to the mother Helen and Marie never met.

The twins spent the first year of their life in the care of nuns at a Catholic orphanage in Omaha. Dad visited them several times a week, and he took us kids with him on many Sundays. When the twins came home to Polk Street, Grandma Strack moved in for many months to help care for them. Mom's sisters Dorothy and Petty, chipped in, too, although they had large families of their own to tend to. Colleen, the twins' oldest sister, shouldered a large share of their care in the early years of their lives. "I did what I had to do," Colleen told me. "It was not a big deal." I disagree. She spent her adolescence as a surrogate mother. That *was* a big deal.

Colleen deflected my praise. "When mom died, Grandma Strack was at our house constantly—cleaning, sweeping, downstairs doing laundry, cooking," she told me. "She stepped in and took care of us. That's one of the reasons that I don't have any bad things to say about her." Our mother's best friends also delivered supper to our house on a rotating schedule. With all this help, from inside and outside of the family, we all somehow managed to survive.

My siblings and I all had a lot of liberty, growing up without a mother. After he lost his packinghouse job during a strike that Cudahy used as excuse to break his union, our father bought a tavern, The Lodge Bar & Café. It was located in LaPlatte, a small town 20 minutes from home, and he worked there day and night to nurture what would become a successful business. As a result, he sometimes lost track of what we were doing at home. Like Colleen, I stormed out of the house a couple of times, stamping my feet and vowing (to myself) to never return. Of course I did return, after spending a night or two at a friend's place. And each time when I got back home, it had not registered with anyone that I'd been gone.

After spending most of the 1960s as a single father, our father found a new love. One day in 1969, he called a family meeting. With his eight children assembled in the front room, he sat down with the beautiful young brunette schoolteacher that he had begun dating, and said to us, "With all of your permission, Beverly and I would like to get married." We all nodded our approval, and a few months later the family trouped up to Beverly Ann Broome's hometown of Rice Lake, Wisconsin, where they were wed on June 14, 1969. Having just turned 27 years old, she committed to being the stepmom of a group of kids ranging in age from 6 to 18, all still deeply scarred by the death of our mother. Bev crafted relationships with each of her husband's children — all while trying to raise her own son, our little brother, Billy, born three years after the wedding. Most importantly, she gave our father a second shot at life, offering emotional stability, abiding love, and deep happiness to a good man who deserved all of that. They are both gone now — Ed Krajicek Sr., the longtime proprietor of the Lodge Bar & Café, died of a heart attack in 1992; Beverly's health gave out in July 2022.

FIFTEEN

Passages and Bus Trips

HARRY STRACK, our lunch pail-toting grandfather, lost his life in 1963, a year after his daughter Helen. His death followed closely his well-deserved retirement. He "smoked like a fiend," as my cousin Mary Dundis Lincoln correctly recalled, and lung cancer got him. The filthy air at the Paxton-Mitchell foundry didn't help: Aunt Petty Keating said her father coughed up a black gummy substance when he got off work. But he also blew about as much smoke as the foundry chimney. I'm sure he snuffed a butt now and then to eat a meal, but I don't recall ever seeing Grandpa Harry without smoke emanating from his mouth, whether from a pipe or a cigarette.

WE ALL WERE LEFT with similar images. When I asked about Grandpa Harry, Nancy Keating Walsh told me, "I remember him as being a very quiet man. He would sit in his rocker in the living room, holding one of his grandkids with a cigarette in his mouth." My sister Colleen recalled that he had a routine that seemed to be designed to get the foundry grime off his body—and out of his throat. "Every time he came home from work, the first thing he did was wash his hands, wash his face, then drink a bottle of beer."

Harry Albert Strack in about 1942

I asked Nancy whether she recalls meeting Harry's half-sister, Cora May Beasley Hamermick, who played such a singular role in his life. May died in Omaha in 1972. Nancy and I would have been in high school then — old enough to have known someone who was so important to our grandfather. Yet I had never heard of May Hamernick before I began this book. This is another example of the validity of my sister Colleen's question: Why didn't we know these people? I was happy to hear from Nancy that Grandma Strack had stayed in touch with May and her daughter, Eva, over the years. "I do remember Grandma talking about May," Nancy told me. "I visited one or both of them [May and her daughter] with Grandma but can't recall much. The name May always comes to mind when I try to recall Grandpa's family."

There's a good reason for that: May was Harry's surrogate parent. I'll remind you that she was the abandoned 7-year-old child living in squalor that sleazy Doc Beasley, her sperm-donor father, was going to visit on his booze-induced death trip by train to Council Bluffs in 1893. And Harry was the little boy whose upbringing was so sketchy that no one in his household could tell a census-taker his correct age, birthdate, or even last name. Yet these half-siblings, by some miracle, went on to become good parents and upright citizens. I have to believe that May was somehow imbued with a strong sense of right and wrong that she passed along to her brother. I'm sorry that I never got a chance to meet her — or thank her.

After Harry died, Grandma Strack sold the S Street house that her parents had built 65 years earlier. She moved into a tidy little place a mile away, at 34th and Washington Streets, close to her good friends Frank and Mary Sack (Lithuanians, of course) and her brother George Strack. This was the house where I was sometimes assigned to keep Grandma company. After she was widowed, she liked to have a grandchild or two around, and I served as the designated companion maybe a half-dozen times, as a seven- or eight-year-old. Her house was almost always quiet — as still as a confessional. Grandma would turn on the radio for a few minutes each morning to listen to a grocery store giveaway contest. Except for the occasional whir of her sewing machine, I heard little else but the relentless ticking of a clock, day and night — tick-tock, tick-tock, tick-tock. And there was no escaping the ticking and tocking: her place on South 34th was the original tiny house — 650 square feet that somehow included two bedrooms, a closet or two, a front room, kitchen, and bathroom. Sixty years later, I get a little claustrophobic just thinking of it. To boot, Grandma and I didn't have much to say to one another. I wish I had known enough to interrupt all that quiet to ask her what the hell *Stole eggs and bought it* meant.

But during a couple of my stays, she took me on unusual mid-morning bus trips to downtown Omaha, miles from home. These journeys did not make much sense to me at the time. I don't recall that she ever bought anything, and she wasn't the sort of adult who would *explain* to a bewildered child what she was up to. But looking back now, I wonder whether Eileen wanted to show her grandson a glimpse of her own youth. I think these trips suggest just how much those formative years working at Hayden Brothers meant to her. With me at her side, we wandered past her old haunts, following a particular route. As I recall, we exited the bus downtown in front of the grand old State Theater, at 14th and Farnam Streets, across from the Paxton Hotel, where her father once worked as a furnace tender. We walked west up to 16th Street and turned north. Descending the sloping street, Grandma slowly window-shopped past the elaborate displays behind vast slabs of plate glass at Brandeis, her old department store competition. While she ogled the displays, I made myself dizzy by stepping back and peering up at the lions growling down from what was a spectacularly ornate building—at least for an unpretentious place like Omaha. Once, we stepped through the grand entrance and stood on Brandeis' main floor for a few moments, Grandma tugging me out of the way of real customers. I think she felt it was something I should see. I must have looked up again. More than the fancy sales counters, I recall the towering ceilings, held aloft by four or five rows of ornate columns. "OK, enough," Grandma Strack soon barked, yanking me back out to the sidewalk. Our tour continued down the same street, past "the dime store" (Woolworth's) to J.C. Penney's, which had moved into the Hayden Brothers building after her old store was shuttered in the late 1930s. We did not dally there, moving swiftly down Dodge Street and back toward the bus stop for our return trip to South Omaha, after perhaps an hour downtown. Our final stop before departing was a particular cafeteria. I don't recall its name or precise location, but the place clearly was meaningful to Grandma. Was it a favorite lunch spot in her years as a shopgirl? Did she meet Harry there? I don't know. But she pointedly paused outside the place during our excursions, peering through the windows. We did not go inside, let alone eat — my greatest pipe dream for these trips. Eileen was far too frugal for that. No, after completing the route, we rode the bus back home, where she would serve me lunch of a glass of milk, half a cheese sandwich on white bread, and a dozen spoonfuls of canned tomato soup.

The frugality aside, this seems like a charming vignette about the water-tossing grandmother whom I have portrayed as a touch sadistic, right? Well, let me add one other detail. The bus fare was a dime. On the first trip, as we stood awaiting the bus on South 36th Street near her home, Grandma swiveled me toward her with a twist of my ear. She held up two dimes, one pinched between the thumb and forefinger of each hand. "Now you look here, David," she said. "Here's your car fare. You put one in the driver's box when you get on, and you hold onto the other so you can get back home. If you lose the second dime, I'm going to leave you downtown. You'll be on your own."

I did not lose that second dime, I can tell you that. I didn't put it in my pocket; that seemed too risky. I clutched it so tightly in the palm of my chubby right hand that it left an impression that seemed to last for days. I may have even drawn a little blood. Like the tossed water, I'm sure that Grandma thought her little dime gag was hilarious. I could be charitable and say it was her way of teaching me to be responsible. It *has* stayed with me in a couple ways, neither having to do with any intended lesson. First, I will gladly drop a wad of paper money into a musician's tip jar or a beggar's palm, but don't even ask for my pocket change: You never know when you might need bus fare. Second, I'll tell you just how deeply this thing is ingrained in my subconscious. For years, I've had a recurring dream in which I am stuck on a bus that travels an endless loop from downtown into my old South Omaha neighborhood. I ring to exit each time it passes near home, but something always goes wrong, and the driver continues on, back toward downtown for another long, tedious loop—my own "protracted sojourn." The dreams are more annoyance than nightmare, but I have an idea that they are enduring residuals from those trips downtown as a boy. So thanks for that, Grandma.

EILEEN STRACK SURVIVED A DOZEN YEARS without Harry. Cancer got her, too. She had a breast removed in the 1950s, and the disease came back around 20 years later. She died on Christmas Day 1975. Nancy Keating Walsh, her most devoted grandchild, was with Grandma Strack nearly every day in her final months. My cousin recalled an interesting vignette from Grandma's funeral that revealed a side of the woman that most of us had not known. Grandma Strack had a favorite nephew, Donald Kleber, son of her older sister, Grace Kinnear Kleber. Donald moved west to California as a young man, but he and Grandma apparently made a point of meeting up at the Q Street bars anytime he visited his large family in Omaha. Stranger still, Aunt Petty Keating told Nancy that when she and Uncle Joe were honeymooning in Colorado Springs in the early 1950s, they were shocked to find her mother and father carousing in the same mountain town with Donald Kleber. On a whim, Harry and Eileen apparently had hopped in their sedan and followed the newlyweds 550 miles to the Rockies—to have a few drinks with Donald, who apparently had hatched the plan for the mountain meetup. They turned around and drove back home the next day.

One more Donald Kleber story from my cousin Nancy: As visitation hour was winding down at Grandma's wake, Nancy watched a stranger arrive with a flourish and stride up to the open casket. She recalls that he was wearing a suit and tie, and he had a drink in his hand — with an airline insignia on the glass. Nancy told me that he clinked his cocktail on Grandma's casket, then said, "Sorry I'm late, Strack. I had a few for us on the plane. Cheers." It was her favorite nephew, just arrived from California to say goodbye. I wish I had known that side of Grandma — and the guy who dared call her "Strack."

MY MOTHER PROVED TO BE the outlier among the Strack kids. Each of the others lived long lives. Bud died in 1997, at age 73. His brother George lived until 80, dying in 2006. Dorothy Dundis left us in 2009, at age 87, and the love of her life, Uncle Al Dundis, joined her in the hereafter in 2018, just two years short of his 100th birthday. (He and I had a final chat about journalism and world events when I visited Omaha while he was in his mid-90s.)

Uncle Joe Keating, a delightful man who always had a joke and a smile for his nieces and nephews, suffered a debilitating stroke while in his 50s. But with the constant aid of his tiny-but-tough wife, he lived for another two decades, dying in 2004 at age 76. And dear Aunt Petty Keating was the last to go. Afflicted with rheumatoid arthritis early in her adult life, she toughed it out for 81 years. Petty died in 2013.

Another generation had passed, and my generation is heading in the same direction, as the oldest of my Strack cousins approach 80. Of course, they all live on in the lifeblood of their children, grandchildren, nieces, and nephews. Many thousands of people around the world can trace their heritage back to the Kinnears of northeast Scotland, the McAuliffes of Ireland, and the Stracks of Germany. The ancestral line did not end with the deaths of Bill and Nellie Kinnear, or Harry and Eileen Strack, or Ed and Helen Krajicek. It goes on forever — until the rivers all run dry and the sun falls from the sky, as an old country ballad puts it.

Ten years ago, when I used 23andMe to analyze my DNA, genetic testing was in its infancy. Using a simple saliva swab sent via mail, 23andMe linked me with other customers who are blood relatives. I was thrilled to discover that a couple dozen of my distant cousins, perfect strangers to me, had also used the firm for DNA analysis. Over the years, this roster of relatives has steadily grown on the 23andMe website. I have found several close cousins as a result, including Rick Kleber, a Californian and nephew of Donald Kleber, Grandma Strack's pal; Joseph Strack of Houston, our Uncle George Strack's youngest son from his first marriage; and even Conrad Krajicek, an Omahan and the grandson of my father's brother.

As of the fall of 2022, 23andMe counts more than 1,500 of my "DNA relatives" among its customers. These people come from 20 different countries. Nearly half (619) are from the United States, not surprisingly. But two dozen live in England, Scotland, or Wales; 16 in Ireland; 13 each in Canada, Italy, and Germany; five each in the Czech Republic, Norway, and Mexico; four in Poland, and a handful from more exotic locales, including Australia and Russia (two each), and a single relative from Trinidad and Tobago, in the

Caribbean. Interestingly, the roster now includes a second person with the surname Strock, a female third cousin who lives in Waco, Texas. This family goes on and on and on—a vast human diaspora that began with two humble, hardworking immigrants. Today, their extended family has grown as big as the boundless sky over Nebraska, their adopted home.

Many of my DNA relatives are fourth or fifth cousins, generally meaning that we share a third or fourth great-grandparent. That may seem like a remote connection, but thanks to this genealogical exploration, I can put a name—or even a face—on many of those people: for example, Nellie McAuliffe Kinnear's grandparents, Patrick O'Malley and Mary (Devane) O'Malley, both born in 1801; or our maternal great-great-grandfather, John Gibler, born in Virginia in 1781 and died in Ohio in 1829; or even William Kinnear's maternal grandmother, Elspeth Hatt Horn, a Scotlander who lived from 1794 until 1844. Does that seem like ancient history? It's not. Here is a photograph of Elspeth that I found on a family tree compiled by a distant relative in Scotland. Do you see any resemblance?

Acknowledgements

THIS BOOK WAS ENRICHED WITH INFORMATION and input from more than a dozen of my cousins and siblings. Thanks, in particular, for the many thoughtful comments and memories from my cousin Nancy Keating Walsh, who offered a trove of information about our grandmother, Eileen Strack. Cousin Mary Dundis Lincoln also added important perspective, and she and her four sisters unearthed a priceless photograph of our great-grandmother, Nellie Kinnear. Colleen Krajicek, my gem of an older sister, contributed several sharp and delightful insights. Thanks to Linda Keating, wife of my dear (older) cousin Nick, for helping to put me in touch with Don Szymanski, a cousin I had never met who generously shared a goldmine of information about our shared kin. Rejean Bogatz Jaksich, my brother Bill's mother-in-law, contributed detective work that helped me tell the story of the fate of one of my great-aunts, Clara Kinnear Bogatz. Special thanks to Loydaine and Tom Strock, a gracious Wyoming couple (and distant cousins) who helped me try to unravel the mystery of my great-grandfather John Strack. Thanks, as always, to Terry Bradshaw, a friend who has designed and shepherded to completion many titles for my publishing imprint, News Ink Books. I especially want to thank my neighbor and friend, Karen Gutliph Graves, a talented artist who contributed the delightful little illustrations sprinkled throughout this book, giving it the touch of whimsy that every book ought to have. And much love goes out to my oldest sibling, Edward Krajicek Jr. After he died a few years ago, we found stacks of his paintings tucked deep inside his closets. I'm very happy to share his railroad painting on the cover of this book. Lastly, thanks to my cousin Mary Beth Keating, who started this project rolling a couple of years ago when she asked, "So when are you going to write a book about Grandma Strack?" Here it is, Mary.

About the Author

DAVID J. KRAJICEK HAS BEEN TELLING STORIES for more than 40 years, as a newspaperman, freelance writer, and author of more than 10 books. A native of South Omaha, Nebraska, he comes from a long line of meatpackers and saloonkeepers — men and women who have told a few stories of their own. A prominent American crime writer, Krajicek wrote a true crime column for the *New York Daily News* for 20 years and appeared frequently on television as a crime expert. He spent a decade as a Columbia University journalism professor and directed a program at Charles University in Prague. He has published widely in leading newspapers and magazines, including *The New York Times* and the *Guardian*. His books include *Mass Killers: Inside the Minds of Men Who Murder; Charles Manson: The Man Who Murdered the Sixties*; the regional best-seller *True Crime: Missouri, The State's Most Notorious Criminal Cases*; his acclaimed first book, *Scooped: Media Miss Real Story on Crime While Chasing Sex, Sleaze, and Celebrities*, and his most recent, a family memoir, *Dear Mama: The Krajicek Boys' Letters to Their Runaway Mother*. Krajicek spent nearly 30 years as bandleader, trombonist, and vocalist for a New York R & B band. He lives in the Catskill Mountains.

www.ingramcontent.com/pod-product-compliance
Lightning Source LLC
Chambersburg PA
CBHW022336280326
41934CB00006B/651